Fundamentals of
Data Science

Take the first Step to Become a
Data Scientist

Step-by-Step Tutorial for Beginners

Samuel Burns

Fundamentals of Data Science : Take the first Step to Become a Data Scientist
Editor: Maria Rica/GlobaltechNTC
Editorial Assistant: Zokolodni Sergey
E-Media Editor: Daniel Soler
Book Design: Rebecca.
Collection : **(Step-by-Step Guide For Beginners)**
Copyright © 2019 by Samuel Burns.

Publisher: **Amazon KDP Printing and Publishing**
Contact: **globaltechntc@bk.ru**
ISBN: 9781693798924
Imprint: Independently published
First Edition: September 2019

CONTENTS

Introduction

The amount of data that is available is increasing every day. These data are stored in both structured and unstructured forms. Some organizations release huge amounts of data every year, even up to terabytes, and hold information that can help the organization make changes and improvements for better customer services and increased profits. The problem is how to extract this information from the data.

With such a vast amount of data, manual processing may not work; thus, a digital means of processing the data is required. "Data science" is used to extract meaningful information from data and use it for decision making, and it is a methodology that is becoming more popular all the time. This is because many organizations have realized that they can enjoy a competitive advantage when they use data for their decision making, particularly as new data analysis tools are being discovered every day for both programmers and non-programmers. This has made it possible for anyone to venture into data science.

Data science is the key to evidence-based decision making. This is because, with data science, decisions can be made based on evidence rather than assumptions. This book introduces you to the fundamentals of data science.

1-Basics of Data Science

What is Data Science?

Data science is a sub-field of Big Data that deals with the extraction of information from raw data. Data science is a combination of computing and statistical techniques used to interpret data so as to make meaningful decisions.

At the core of data science is data. This is raw information generated by businesses. The data can be in a structured, semi-structured, or unstructured form. Mining such amounts of data to identify trends and patterns can help an organization improve its efficiency, identify new market opportunities, rein in costs, and increase its competitive advantage. The role of data science is to process this data to gain business value from it.

Data science employs fields such as statistics, mathematics, and computer science disciplines, and utilizes techniques such as cluster analysis, machine learning, and visualization. Data science continues to evolve as one of the most in-demand and promising paths for skilled professionals.

Data science has been made easy by the increasingly huge amounts of data. Every organization is generating data on a daily basis. There are numerous ways and platforms from which we can get data including cell phones, e-commerce sites, social media, internet searches, healthcare surveys, etc. The production of huge amounts of data has led to a new field of study called "Big Data," which refers to the vast stores of data that can be analyzed to produce better operational tools that can be applied in sectors such as finance, transport, regulation, and manufacturing.

Steps in Data Science

The following steps help you identify patterns, draw conclusions, and make predictions on a particular set of data:

1. Problem definition

In data mining, you have to define your problem and determine how the data can be used to provide answers to the problem. You also have to define the objectives to be achieved at the end.

2. Data preparation

In this step, you should consolidate and then clean the data. The data may be scattered all over the organization and stored in different formats, or it may have some inconsistencies such as missing or wrong entries. In data cleaning, you have to remove the bad data, interpolate the missing values, find the hidden data correlations, identify the accurate sources of data, and determine the best columns to be used for data analysis.

3. Data exploration

The prepared data are explored in this step. This calls for you to understand the data appropriately so as to create the best model. During data exploration, you have to calculate the maximum and minimum values, calculate the mean and the standard deviations, and determine how the data are distributed. This will help you identify any flaws in the data and fix them before you can create the model.

4. Building the models

This step involves creating the data mining model or models. The knowledge gained from the previous step will help you do this. The mining structure will help you determine the data columns that are used for data mining. You have to link the structure to the data source. Once the mining structure has been processed, the Analysis Services will generate the aggregates as well as other useful information that can be used for data analysis. The model usually has attribute specifications that will be used as inputs to the model, attributes to be predicted, and the parameters to instruct the algorithm on how to process the data.

5. Exploration and validation of the models

This step involves the validation of the constructed model so as to determine its effectiveness. Before you can deploy any model into a production environment, you have to test how well it performs. It is also good to always create different models with different configurations and then determine the one with the best performance.

6. Deploying and updating the models

The model that yields the best performance should now be deployed into the production environment. Once the model is in the production environment, you can use it to perform any task required. The model can help you make predictions, create statistical queries, etc.

What are Data, Datasets?

Data comprise a collection of facts in the form of numbers, measurements, words, observations, or descriptions of things. Data are normally formatted in a certain way, e.g., as text or numbers on a piece of paper, as bytes and bits stored in an electronic memory, or as facts stored in the mind of a person. Since the 1990s, people have been using the term *data* to refer to information stored in computers.

The term *data* is the plural form for the noun *datum*, which is a single piece of information. With the advancement in technology, a number of terms have been used to describe data. Let us define examples of these terms and phrases:

- **Big data** - this is a massive volume of structured and unstructured data so large that it is difficult to process using traditional software and database technologies.
- **Raw data** - this is data that has been collected but has not been analyzed or formatted.
- **Structured data** - this is data resides in a fixed field within a file or record. It includes data contained in spreadsheets and relational databases.

- **Unstructured data** - this is data that is not residing in traditional row–column databases. It is the opposite of structured data.

A *dataset* is a collection of discrete, related items of related data that can be accessed individually or managed as a whole entity. A dataset is usually organized into a type of data structure. We may, for example, have a dataset in a database that contains a collection of employees' data including employee names, date of employment, age, salary, department, etc. Such a database can be considered to be a dataset because the bodies of data in it are related.

History of Data Science

The process of extracting hidden connections from data for prediction purposes has a long history. The term "data science" was not known until the 1990s. Its foundation is made up of three scientific disciplines:

- **Statistics** - the numeric study of relationships between data.
- **Artificial intelligence** - human-like intelligence displayed by machines and software.
- **Machine learning** - algorithms capable of learning from data in order to make predictions.

The increasing complexity of datasets and the power of technology have made data science evolve from static data delivery to proactive and dynamic information deliveries. In the late 1980s, the term **"data science"** began to gain popularity within the research community by data analysts, management information system (MIS) communities, and statisticians.

In the early 1990s, data science was known to be a step or a sub-process of a larger process known as Knowledge Discovery in Databases (KDD). KDD can be defined as the nontrivial process of identifying novel, valid, potentially useful, and understandable patterns in data.

Data science became very popular in the 1990s due to dedicated conferences, rapid development in technology, faster computers, and improved data storage capabilities. These made it possible for organizations to store data in a computer-readable form and to process large volumes of data using desktop computers.

By the end of the 1990s, data mining had become a popular technique used by organizations. The introduction of customer loyalty cards made it possible for organizations to record customer purchases—data that could be mined to reveal customer purchasing patterns. The popularity of data mining has grown rapidly over the last decade.

For some time, data science focused on tabular data. However, with the evolvement in technology, there was a need to mine data from different sources. This led to the emergence of the following:

- **Text mining** - this remains a popular data mining activity. It clusters or categorizes large document collections like web pages and news articles. It is also applied in opinion mining where useful information is obtained from data presented in a questionnaire style.
- **Image mining** - this involves the application of data

mining techniques to both 2D and 3D images.

- **Graph mining** - a data science technique focused on data represented in a graph structure. It is applied in problem domains such as computer networks, chemical reactions, bioinformatics, social networks, and program flow structures.

In the last two decades, data mining has become very popular as a discipline in its own. Today, data science is used in businesses, government, science, and other fields.

2-Decision Theory

Decision theory is an interdisciplinary approach that deals with determining how decisions are made in an uncertain environment and when some variables are unknown. Some of the disciplines combined in decision theory include psychology, philosophy, statistics, and mathematics.

Decision makers in organizations of all sizes are faced with serious dilemmas and most decision makers do not have the time to educate themselves about a number of subjects. They are only in need of clear and distilled information that can help them make informed decisions quickly. This information can be obtained by employing the right data science skills.

Data is the key to evidence-based decision making. An organization that uses its data for decision making can enjoy a competitive advantage over its competitors. Research has shown that leaders who rely on data to make decisions make 12% more revenue that those who do not. However, for this to be the case, one needs to know how to use big data effectively.

Let us discuss the four types of data analytics that are good for decision making.

Descriptive Analytics

The purpose of descriptive statistics is to answer the question, ***what happened?*** This involves gathering data from multiple sources to know more about the past. However, such data will only tell that something is right or wrong but it won't explain why. For example, a retailer will be able to tell the average sales volume for a month, a hospital will tell the number of patients that were admitted, etc. This means that a company that is highly data-driven will not only focus on descriptive analytics but it will combine it with other types of analytics.

Diagnostic Analytics

It is possible to measure historical data against other data so as to answer the question, *why did it happen?* Diagnostic analytics provides us with an opportunity to drill down to identify patterns and find out dependencies. Companies should apply diagnostic analytics because it provides deep insights into certain problems. However, a company must have access to a substantive amount of information; otherwise, data collection will become time-consuming.

For example, a retailer can scrutinize gross profit and sales to categories so as to tell why he did not achieve the target net profit.

Predictive Analytics

Predictive analytics answers, *what is likely to happen?* It relies on the findings from descriptive and diagnostic analytics to detect clusters, tendencies, and exceptions, and then predict future trends, thus making predictive analytics a good tool for forecasting. Predictive analytics is associated with numerous benefits, but it is good for you to know now that forecasting just gives us an estimate and accuracy is highly dependent on data quality and stability. This means that careful treatment and continuous optimization are required.

Predictive analytics brings about a proactive approach. A company may, for example, know the number of customers who are about to reduce their spending and, thus, run targeted marketing activities so as to remediate this loss. A company can also assess its cash flow and know the risk of investing in expansion.

Prescriptive Analytics

The work of prescriptive analytics is to prescribe the necessary actions needed to eliminate a possible future problem or take advantage of a promising trend. A good example of prescriptive analytics is when a company identifies opportunities for repeat purchases after analyzing customer data and sales history.

With prescriptive analytics, we need both historical data as well as external data due to the nature of statistical algorithms. This type of analytics also relies on more advanced tools compared with other types of analytics, such as machine learning, algorithms, and business rules, making it a bit more sophisticated for implementation and management. This means that before a company implements prescriptive analytics, it has to perform a comparison between the required effort and the expected value.

Each company needs all the above types of analytics at

different stages of decision making. This is because a combination of these is required for a company to make informed decisions. However, it doesn't mean that a company has to use all four types of analytics for each decision. The type of analytics that a company chooses to use will depend on the depth of analysis required for the task. However, it is very clear that the majority of companies are in need of advanced data analytics for more informed decision making.

3-Estimation Theory

Estimation theory deals with the precision and accuracy of values that you can count, measure, or calculate. It gives you a way of indicating how precise your measurements are and to calculate an appropriate measurement range that is more likely to include the true value.

One of the major tasks in statistics is to estimate the value of an unknown population parameter. For example, a poll may be conducted to determine the number of male adults in a particular city who are unemployed. The process used to provide values to the unknown population's parameter is referred to as *estimation*.

When you measure or estimate a value, both the measured and estimated values will differ from the truth in two different ways; that is, they can be *inaccurate, imprecise*, or both. Let us discuss the meaning of these two measurement attributes:

- Accuracy is how close the measurement is to the true value without a systematic bias in one direction or another.
- Precision is how close the bunch of replicate measurements comes to one another, that is, how reproducible they are.

Basic Terminologies

The following are the basic terminologies used in estimation theory:

- **Population** - This is a group of individuals under study. The population can be either finite or infinite. For example, all registered voters in the USA.

- **Sample** - This is a finite subset of individuals obtained from a population. A good example is when you select some voters from all registered voters in the USA.

- **Parameter** - This is a statistical constant of a population. Examples of such constants are the mean, variance, standard deviation, etc. For example, the mean age of all registered voters in USA.

- **Statistic** – This is a statistical constant of a sample such as mean, variance, etc. This means that any function of a random sample $x_1, x_2, ..., x_n$ being observed, for example, T_n is called a "statistic." For example, the mean income of the selected voters.

- **Estimator** - If we use a statistic to estimate an unknown parameter, say θ, of distribution, then it is referred to as an estimator. For example, "sample mean" is an estimator of the population mean.

- **Estimate** - The value of an estimator is known as an estimate of an unknown parameter. For example, the mean income of selected voters is $2500, which represents the mean income of all registered voters.

- **Sampling distribution** - After the total probability has been distributed according to the value of the statistic, we say that the distribution is sampling distribution.

For example, if we need to know the average height of a voter, we can select some voters randomly then use the sample mean to estimate the population mean.

- **Standard error-** This is the standard deviation of the sampling distribution of a statistic and is denoted by *s.e.* For example, if we need to get the variability of voters' height, then we can calculate the standard error.

What is Good Estimator?

It is good for you to know what a good estimator is. A true estimator is one that is as close to the correct value of the parameter as possible. The following criteria can be used to determine whether an estimator is good.

Unbiasedness

Unbiasedness is a very desirable property of a good estimator. An estimator, say T_n, is said to be an unbiased estimator of $\gamma (\theta)$, with $\gamma (\theta)$ being a function of an unknown parameter θ, if the expectation of the estimator equals to the population parameter. This can be expressed as shown in the following equation:

$$E [Tn] = \gamma (\theta)$$

Consistency

An estimator is consistent if an increase in sample size returns an estimate with a smaller standard error, that is, the standard deviation of the sampling distribution of a statistic. If the size of the sample is increased, then it almost becomes certain that the value of the statistic will be close to the correct value of the parameter.

Efficiency

We need a further criterion that will help us choose between estimators while relying on the common property of consistency. Such a criterion based on the variances of a sampling distribution of estimators is called **"efficiency."**

It is the size of the standard error for the statistic. If we compare two statistics from a sample of a similar size, then we decide on the one to be a good estimator, the statistic with a smaller standard deviation or the standard error of the sampling distribution.

Sufficiency

We say an estimator is sufficient for a parameter if it has all the information in the sample about the parameter.

Point Estimation Methods

You are now aware of the requisites of a good estimator. We now need to go deeper and discuss the various ways through which we can obtain such estimators.

Method of Moments (MoM)

This method involves equating population moments, which is, means, variances of theoretical models, to the corresponding sample moments, that is, the means and variances of the observed sample data, and then solve for the parameter(s).

Method of Maximum Likelihood Estimation (MLE)

This is known to be the best method for finding estimators. The MLE usually has asymptotic properties that are easy to find and they are very good when it comes to large samples. The term *asymptotic* means that the samples are very large.

The goal of this approach is to find a value θ that will most likely give us a particular sample, that is, to find the value of θ that will maximize the likelihood function.

Method of Minimum Variance

This method is also referred to as *Minimum Variance Unbiased Estimator (MVUE).* Just as the name suggests, it gives an estimator that is unbiased and has minimum variance.

If we have a statistic T_n that is based on a sample of size n in such a way that

- T_n is unbiased and
- T_n has the smallest variance among the class of all unbiased estimators,

Then we call T_n an **MVUE** of θ.

4-Coordinate Systems

Data usually comprises an array of numbers. Spatial data are similar, although these data have some numerical information that you can use to position it somewhere on the Earth. Such numbers are part of coordinate system that provides you with a frame of reference for your data so as to locate the different features on the surface of the Earth, align your data to the other data, create maps, and perform spatially accurate analyses.

All spatial data are created in the form of a coordinate system, whether it is lines, polygons, points, annotation, or rasters. There are different ways through which we can specify the coordinates such as feet, decimal degrees, meters, or kilometers. Note that we can use any form of measurement as a coordinate system. Identification of the measurement system should be the first step when choosing the type of coordinate system to use for displaying data in its correct position relative to the other data.

Data are defined using both vertical and horizontal coordinate systems. Vertical coordinate systems are used for locating the relative depth or height of data while horizontal coordinate systems are used for locating data across the surface of the Earth.

Horizontal coordinate systems are of three types:

- Geographic
- Projected
- Local

To know the coordinate system to which your data belongs, you only have to observe each layer's properties.

Geographic Coordinate System

The geographic coordinate systems (GCS) mostly use units of decimal degrees to measure the degrees of longitude (*x*-coordinate) and latitude (*y*-coordinate). Data location is expressed using either positive or negative numbers; that is, positive x and y values for north of the equator and east of the prime meridian, and negative values for south of the equator and west of the prime meridian.

Projected Coordinate System

This is another type of coordinate system that can be used for expressing spatial data. Coordinates are expressed using linear measurements instead of angular degrees. These types of coordinate systems are also known as *map projections.*

The projected coordinate system is known to have constant

lengths, angles, and areas across the two dimensions unlike what we have in other types of coordinate systems. The locations are identified by the use of *x,y* coordinates on a grid and the origin are the center of the grid. Each position is identified by two values that identify its position from the origin.

Local Coordinate System

Some data may be expressed in a local coordinate system with false origin (0,0 or others) in an arbitrary location that can be anywhere on the Earth. This type of coordinate system is normally used in the large-scale mapping. The false origin can be aligned to a real-world coordinate or not, but for purposes of data capture, distances and bearings may be measured using a local coordinate system instead of global coordinates.

Projections

A projection is a way of displaying the coordinate system and data on a flat surface like a digital screen or a piece of paper. Mathematical operations are used for conversion of the coordinate system that is used on the earth's curved surface to one for a flat surface.

Because there exists no perfect way of transposing a curved surface to a flat surface without distortion, there are different map projections that offer different properties. Some will preserve the curved shape, whereas others will preserve the distance, area, or direction. The location, extent, and the property that you need to preserve will determine the kind of map projection that you choose.

T r a n s f o r m a t i o n s

Once you have defined a coordinate system matching your data, you may still be in need of using data in a different coordinate system. Transformations become useful in this case. Transformations are needed to convert data between different vertical coordinate systems or between different geographic coordinate systems. If your data does not line up, then you will face inaccuracies and difficulties in the analysis and the mapping that you perform on the mismatched data.

5-Linear Transformations

After creating a residual plot, we may realize that our data are nonlinear. However, it is possible for us to transform this and make it more linear. It is after this that we will be able to use linear regression techniques on the nonlinear data.

To transform a variable, we use a mathematical operation so as to change its measurement scale. In a linear transformation, the linear relationship between the variables is maintained. This means that for variables x and y, their relationship will remain intact even after the transformation. An example of a linear transformation is multiplying x with a constant, dividing x by a constant, and adding a constant to x.

After applying a linear transformation to a random variable, a new variable is created. Let us demonstrate this using an example.

Suppose we have X, a random variable, and m and b are constants. The following example shows how a linear transformation of variable X creates a new random variable Y.

- Adding a constant: $Y = X + \mathbf{b}$
- Subtracting a constant: $Y = X - \mathbf{b}$
- Multiplying by a constant: $Y = \mathbf{m}X$
- Dividing by a constant: $Y = X/\mathbf{m}$
- Multiplying by a constant then adding a constant: $Y = \mathbf{m}X + \mathbf{b}$
- Dividing by a constant then subtracting a constant: $Y = X/\mathbf{m} - \mathbf{b}$

Note: Suppose W and X are variables, and the two have a correlation that is equal to r. If a new variable, say Y, is created after applying a linear transformation on X, then the correlation between Y and Z will remain equal to r.

Reasons for Transformation

Let us discuss the various reasons as to why we do transformations:

1. Convenience

When a scale is transformed, it becomes more convenient for a certain purpose. For example, percentages instead of original data, sines instead of degrees.

A good example of a transformation is standardization in which we adjust the values for differing level and spread. Through standardization, we can compare values that have been expressed in different units.

2. Reducing skewness

We can use a transformation for the purpose of reducing skewness. A symmetric distribution, or one that is close to being symmetrical, is easier to analyze than a skewed distribution. A normal distribution is preferred because it fits with many statistical methods.

3. Linear relationships

When it comes to relationships between variables, it is easier to deal with linear than curved relationships. This is mostly the case when dealing with linear regression.

4. Equal spreads

We can use a transformation to create spreads that are approximately equal. This can be done even when there is marked variation in level. This will make the data easy for analysis and interpretation.

Steps in Linear Transformation

The following are the necessary steps for anyone conducting a linear transformation:

- Perform a standard regression analysis on your raw data.
- Create a residual plot.

- If the plot pattern is random, don't transform the data.
- If the plot pattern isn't random, continue.
- Calculate the coefficient of determination (R^2).
- Transform the independent variable, dependent variable, or both.
- Perform a regression analysis using the transformed variables.
- Calculate the coefficient of determination (R^2) depending on the transformed variables.
- If you find that the transformed R^2 is greater than raw-score R^2, then your transformation was successful.

Common Transformations

There are different types of transformations that we can apply on data. Note that transformations should only be used over ranges that can yield real numbers as results. Here are the common types of transformations applied to data.

Reciprocal

The reciprocal, **a to 1/a,** with its converse, the negative reciprocal, **a to −1/a,** is a very strong transformation that greatly affects the shape of the distribution. Reciprocals cannot be applied to zero values. It is true that the reciprocal can be applied to negative values, but it will not be useful unless all values are positive.

We can interpret the reciprocal of a ratio as the ratio itself. For example:

- Population density (people per unit area) will become area per person.
- Students per teacher will become teachers per student.
- Rates of erosion will become time to erode a unit depth.

The reciprocal works by reversing the order in values with a similar sign, that is, the largest becomes the smallest, etc. When a negative reciprocal is used, the order of the values will be preserved.

Logarithm

This type of transformation also has a great impact on the shape of a distribution. It can be read as the logarithm *a* to log base **10** of *a* to log base e (natural logarithm) of *an* (**ln** *a*) or to log base **2** of *a*. This can be used when you need to reduce the right-skewness for measured variables. We can apply it on zero or negative values. A unit on the logarithmic scale is a multiplication by the base of the logarithms that have been used.

Consider the following decline or exponential growth:

```
y = a exp(bx)
```

The following transformation can make the above exponential growth linear:

```
ln y = ln a + bx
```

After the above transformation, the response variable y will be logged.

Cube Root

This is a strong transformation with a great impact on the shape of a distribution. The cube root is a to $a\wedge(1/3)$. However, compared with the logarithm transformation, it is weaker. We can use it to reduce right-skewness and it also brings an advantage in that it can be applied to negative and zero values. The cube root of a volume will have the units of a length. This type of transformation is mostly applied when dealing with rainfall data.

A special operation is required when applying this transformation to negative values. For example, consider the following:

(3)(3)(3) = 27

    and

(-3)(-3)(-3) = -27.

From the above example, we can say that the cube root of a negative number has a negative sign and the same absolute value as the cube root of the equivalent positive number.

This property is also true in any other root whose power is the reciprocal of an odd positive integer, that is, powers of **1/3, 1/5, 1/7**, etc.

S q u a r e   R o o t

This type of transformation has a moderate impact on the distribution of a shape. It can be read as *a to $a^{(1/2)}$ = sqrt(a).* However, it is weaker when compared with the logarithm and cube root transformations. We can use the square root transformation to reduce right-skewness and it has an advantage in that we can apply it on zero values.

The square root takes the units of the length. It is good for counted data when the values are few.

S q u a r e

This type of transformation has a moderate effect on the shape of the distribution and it can be used for reducing left-skewness. We use it to fit a response using a quadratic function *y = a + b x + c x^2.*

Quadratics are characterized by a turning point, which can be either a minimum or maximum. However, the turning point in a function fitted on data may be far beyond the observation limits.

The distance of a body from the origin is said to be quadratic if the body is moving under constant acceleration, giving a clear physical justification for using a quadratic. In other cases, we use quadratics solely because they are able to mimic a relationship within the data region. Outside the region, they may have very poor performance because they take on arbitrarily large values for extreme values of x and unless we constrain the intercept a to be 0, they may have an unrealistically close performance to the origin.

The type of transformation to use will depend on the nature of the data that you have. In all cases, the goal should be to maintain the linear relationship between the values.

6-Graph Theory

Visualizations provide us with a powerful way of discovering and displaying the patterns hidden in data. Any time you are working with a set of new data, it will be good for you to explore it by creating the necessary visualizations. The use of graphs is a great visualization technique. Graphs can help a business explore their data and make better business decisions. However, before understanding how to use graphs, you have to understand the fundamentals underlying them, that is, graph theory.

A graph is simply a combination of vertices and edges. The vertices are also known as *nodes*. You can tell that in a graph the vertices/nodes are the points while edges are the connections. Two nodes in a graph that are connected to each other by an edge are said to be *adjacent* to each other.

Fundamentals of Graphs

There are many terms that you should be familiar with when working with graphs. They include the following:

- **Vertex** - this is a point where many multiple lines meet. It is also referred to as a *node* and denoted using an alphabet letter.
- **Edge** - a line connecting two vertices and denoted by a line.
- **Graph** - this is a combination of vertices and edges and denoted as G = (V, E), where V is the set of vertices in the graph and E is the set of edges in the graph.
- **Degree of vertex** - this is the number of edges that are connected to a vertex and denoted as degree of vertex A, deg(A) = 2.
- **Parallel edge** - these are vertices that are connected by more than one edge.
- **Multi graph** - a type of graph that has parallel edges.

Types of Graphs

There are different types of graphs. Here are the most popular types of graphs:

- **Null graphs** - these are graphs without edges. They are only made up of vertices represented using alphabet letters. There are no connections between the vertices.

- **Non-directed graphs** - these are graphs with edges, but the direction of the edges is not indicated. A good example of this type of graph is when you add someone to your friend list on Facebook. You will also be added to their friend list. Such a two-way relationship will create a non-directed graph.

- **Directed graphs** - these are graphs with edges and the direction of the edges is indicated using arrows. A good example is when you follow someone on Twitter. They may not follow you back, creating a one-way relationship, which is a directed graph.

- **Connected graph** - this is a graph in which there is no unreachable vertex, that is, there is a path between every pair of vertices.

- **Disconnected graphs** - these are graphs with an unreachable vertex(s), that is, there is no path between every pair of vertices.

For the case of a connected graph, a path always exists from every vertex to all other vertices of the graph.

For an unconnected graph, there is at least one vertex without connections to all other vertices of the graph. This can be applied in the airline industry because airlines can be able to tell whether all the airports are connected or not.

- **Regular graph** - when graph vertices have the same degree, such graphs are said to be k-regular graphs, with k being the degree of any graph vertex.

Graph Traversal

Graph traversal is the process of navigating through the graph to find nodes. It involves visiting each vertex and edge exactly once in a defined order. Because each vertex should be visited only once, we have to take note of the vertices that have been traversed so that no vertex is traversed more than once. Let us discuss the most popular graph traversal methods.

Breadth First Search

In this method, we start from the root/source node and traverse the graph in a layer-wise manner. Here are the steps for a breadth first search:

1. First, move horizontally to visit all nodes of the current layer.
2. Then, move to the next layer and repeat the first step.

This means that we begin with the root node and then move downwards to Layer 1, which is the first layer. We then move horizontally so as to traverse all the nodes of that layer. Once done with that layer, we move to the next layer and repeat the above steps. These steps are repeated until all the layers and vertices have been covered.

The main advantage of this type of traversal is that we will always find the shortest path that leads to the goal. It is good for use when we have small graphs and trees but inappropriate for complex graphs. In complex graphs, it will take too much time for us to find the goal and a large amount of memory is required. Let us discuss another graph traversal method that requires a smaller amount of memory that the breadth-first search.

Depth First Search

This graph traversal method involves the following steps:

1. First, select the root node then store all of its adjacent nodes.

2. Then, select a node from the list of stored nodes and again store all of its adjacent nodes.

3. Repeat these steps until we have no available node.

After a full exploration of a path, we are allowed to remove it from the memory. This means that the depth first search is only required to store the root node, all the children of the root node, and its current position. We can use it to overcome memory shortage problems associated with the breadth first search.

Binary Search Tree

In this method, all tree nodes are arranged in sorted order. This arrangement is done based on a condition. It is a very fast approach and requires less memory to complete.

To use it, we create a condition. The traversal is done to the node that meets the condition.

7-Algorithms

In data science, an algorithm is a set of calculations and heuristics that can create a model from your data. The algorithm has to analyze the data provided so as to identify any trends or patterns. A number of iterations have to be made so as to determine the optimal parameters that can be used for model building. The parameters then have to be applied to the whole dataset so as to obtain detailed statistics and actionable patterns.

Let us now discuss some of the common algorithms used in data science.

Regression Algorithms

Regression analysis is a type of predictive modeling with the aim of finding the relationship between a dependent or the target variable and the independent or predictor variable. It is a good technique for time-series modeling, forecasting, and finding relationships between variables. For example, you can use regression analysis to determine the relationship between overloading and the number of road accidents.

How Regression Algorithms Work

Regression is a good technique for one to model and analyzes data. In most cases, a curve or a line is drawn for the data points with the aim of reducing the distance between these data points. To make it simple, the purpose of regression is to find and estimate the distance or relationship between two or more variables.

For example, suppose you need to determine how the sales of a company have grown with the changes in the economic conditions. Recent company data show two and one-half times growth in company sales than in the economy. With this, we can predict the future sales of the company because we have past data of the company.

With regression analysis, it is also possible for us to determine the impact of variables measured on different scales. Examples include the impact of price changes and promotional activities. With such knowledge, data scientists, data analysts, and market researchers can know the variables to eliminate and the ones to use in building predictive models.

Linear Regression

This is statistical modeling used for modeling the relationship between a particular explanatory variable and the dependent variable. The observed data points have to be fitted on some linear equation. An example is when you need to model the BMI of individuals by using their weight.

Linear regression can help one determine whether there exists a relationship or a significant association between your variables. The checking can be done by use of scatter plots.

A linear regression line usually takes the line given below:

```
Y = a + bX,
```

in which X = explanatory variable,

Y = dependent variable,

b = slope of the line,

a = intercept (the value of y when x = 0).

The Least Squares Method (LSM) can help us get the best fit line and can help us fit the best regression line. It works by minimizing the sum of the squares of vertical deviations from each data point to our line. Because all deviations have to be squared, negative and positive values will not cancel each other. The R-squared method can also be used for assessing the performance of the model.

Logistic Regression

This method helps us find the probability of failure (probability = failure) and the probability of success (probability = success) for an event. This algorithm should only be used when the dependent variable takes binary values, that is, true/false, 0/1, etc.

The *Y* values should range between 0 and 1 and they take the following equation:

```
Odds = p/ (1-p) = probability of occurrence /
probability of not occurring
ln(odds) = ln(p/(1-p))
logit(p) = ln(p/(1-p)) = b0+b1X1+b2X2+b3X3....+bkXk
```

In the above equation, *p* represents the probability of the presence of a characteristic of interest. This algorithm is widely used in classification problems. For you to avoid the problems of over fitting and under fitting, ensure that all the significant variables have been included. Large sample sizes are also required for this algorithm as maximum likelihood estimates are less powerful in cases of low sample sizes compared with the ordinary least squares method.

When to Apply Regression Algorithms

Regression is a good technique when one needs to know the factors that matter most and the ones that should be ignored. Regression can also help you understand how various factors interact with one another.

Regression algorithms are highly applied in businesses and companies to determine what they can do to impact sales and retain their employees or recruit the best employees.

Companies are also using regression algorithms to predict future events.

K - N e a r e s t   N e i g h b o r s   (K N N)   A l g o r i t h m

KNN is a simple algorithm that works well in practical situations. The algorithm is non-parametric, meaning that no assumption is made regarding the underlying distribution of your data. The algorithm can be applied in both regression and classification problems.

How KNN Works

In KNN, complex data structures such as $k-d$ trees can be used for data storage. This helps to make look-ups and matching for the discovery of new patterns during predictions.

Once you have stored the whole of the data training set, you should consider the data's consistency. Update it after getting new data, then make sure that any erroneous data are removed.

For KNN to make predictions, it directly uses the dataset. The predictions are made for some new instance (x) by a search through the whole training set for K similar instances (neighbors) and the output variable is summarized for the K instances. In the case of regression, this can be a mean output variable, whereas, for a classification problem, this can be mode class variable or the most common.

To determine the K instances in a training dataset which are similar to the new input, we use a distance measure. For input variables that are real values, the common distance measure is the Euclidean distance. To calculate this distance, we have to find the square root of the sum of squared differences between new point (X) and the existing point (Xi) across all the input variables j. This can be expressed using the following formula:

```
EuclideanDistance(x, xi) = sqrt( sum( (xj - xij)^2 )
)
```

Other distances that can be used include the following:

- **Hamming distance** - involves the calculation of the distance between the binary vectors.

- **Manhattan distance** - involves the calculation of the distance between the real vectors by use of the sum of their absolute difference. It is also referred to as "City Block Distance."

- **Minkowski distance** - this is a generalization of the above two distances.

The kind of distance to use should be determined by your data. If you are not sure of the best distance for you to use, then just experiment with the different distance measures and different values for K and choose the one that yields the most accurate model.

Euclidian distance should be used where the input variables are of a similar type, for example, all measures are heights and widths. The Manhattan distance should be used where the input variables are of different types, for example, age, height, gender, etc.

To find the value of K, just tune the algorithm. It is always good for you to try different values for K then choose the one that yields the best model.

KNN's computational complexity normally increases with the

size of the dataset. If the training dataset is too large, then you can make KNN stochastic by taking some sample from your training dataset from where you will calculate K-most similar instances.

If the KNN algorithm is used for a regression problem, then the prediction will be based on the median or mean of K-most similar instances.

When KNN is used for a classification problem, the output may be calculated as the class that has the highest frequency from K-most similar instances. Every instance will vote for their class and the class with the most votes will be taken for prediction.

The calculation of class probabilities can be done as the normalized frequency of the samples that belong to every class in a set of K similar instances for the new data.

When to Apply KNN

Although the KNN algorithm can be applied to both classification and regression problems, it is widely applied to classification problems. Whenever you need to determine the similarity between your variables, KNN is the best algorithm to use.

It is a good algorithm for use in pattern recognition and statistical estimation.

Clustering Algorithms

Clustering is simply the process of dividing the data points into groups known as "clusters" such that the data points in the same cluster are more related compared with their relationship with data points in the other clusters. In simple terms, the goal of clustering is to segregate groups with similar characteristics and then assign them to clusters. From this, it is very clear that clustering is the most important unsupervised learning algorithm. The goal of clustering is to find the structure in a collection of unlabeled data. The members of each cluster are similar in some way.

How Clustering Works

Suppose you run a rental store and your aim is to know the preferences of your customers in order to boost your business. It is impossible for you to analyze the preferences of each customer and then arrive at a strategy for each of them. The best way to approach this is to divide your customers into a number of groups, say eight, according to their purchasing habits. A strategy should then be devised for each group of customers. This is how clustering algorithms work.

Clustering can either be hard or soft. For the case of hard clustering, every data point must belong to a particular group completely or not. In our above example, each customer must belong to any one of the eight groups. In soft clustering, each data point is not put into a separate cluster; instead, the likelihood or probability of assigning that data point to the cluster is assigned. In our above example, every customer is assigned a probability of belonging to one of the eight groups.

K Means Clustering Algorithm

K Means is a clustering algorithm that works iteratively with the aim of finding the local maxima during each iteration. The algorithm follows the following steps:

i.   Specify the number of clusters you wish to have (K).
ii. Assign each data point to a cluster randomly.
iii. Determine the cluster centroids.
iv. Re-assign each point to the closest cluster centroid.
v.   Re-compute the cluster centroids.
vi. Repeat steps 4 and 5 until there are no possible improvements. These steps should be repeated until you have reached the global optima. That will be the end of the algorithm if it was not stated explicitly.

The K Means clustering algorithm offers fast computation if the variables are huge and K is kept small. The algorithm can produce tighter clusters, making it easy for one to determine the relationship between the variables in the cluster.

Hierarchical Clustering

This clustering algorithm works by creating a hierarchy of clusters. The algorithm begins with all data points that have been assigned to their own cluster. The two nearest clusters are then merged into a single cluster. The algorithm will terminate once only a single cluster is left. A dendrogram is the best way to demonstrate how this clustering algorithm works. In a dendrogram, you begin with a set of data points with each assigned to separate clusters. The two closest clusters are merged and this continues until we remain with one cluster at the top of the dendrogram. The height in a dendrogram at which any two clusters are merged shows the distance between the two clusters in a data space.

Note that K Means is suitable when you have big data. This is because the K Means algorithm has a linear time complexity, whereas the hierarchical clustering algorithm has quadratic time complexity. In K Means, the number of clusters is chosen randomly, meaning that the results obtained may differ after running the algorithm multiple times. In hierarchical clustering, we may reproduce the results.

The following are areas in which you can apply clustering algorithms:

- Market segmentation
- Medical imaging
- Search result grouping
- Image segmentation
- Recommendation engines
- Anomaly detection
- Social network analysis

When to Use Clustering Algorithms

Clustering algorithms should be used when one has a set of items and there is a need to create a number of groups from these items. Items that are similar are placed in the same group while the different items are placed in different groups. A good example is when you want to group a number of people as either male or female. You can use their characteristics such as hair length. If the difference in the hair length between individuals is less, then they will be grouped together. Suppose you have a number of news articles and you need to group them so that you may have business articles together, politics articles together, etc. This is another area you can apply clustering algorithms.

Suppose you have a number of documents written in different languages. You can use clustering algorithms to create clusters from these documents based on the language the documents are written in.

Artificial Neural Networks

Neurons in the human brain are interconnected to form a network like semiconductors in a computer processor. Each neuron interacts with surrounding neurons following a set of defined rules.

An artificial neuron is a software simulation of how the human brain works. It is a network of interconnected programs (neurons). Once the data have entered the neural network, operations are performed on it by the first neuron and the output will be determined by how the neuron has been programmed to handle data with those attributes. This data is passed to the next neuron on the network and operation is done on the data. The neurons in an artificial neural network are arranged in layers and the output is produced in the final layer.

The process of turning input into output is the result of programming the individual neurons through which the data pass as well the starting conditions of the data. To make it simple, artificial neural networks are a brain simulation. Rules can be implemented in artificial neural networks so as to ensure that they simulate how the human brain works.

How Artificial Neural Networks Work

The process of learning in neural networks is implemented by using a learning algorithm. The neurons in a neural network are organized into layers. Each layer is connected to the layers on either side. The purpose of the input layer is to receive input from the external environment that you need to learn about. The last layer in the neural network is referred to as the output layer and this is the layer that gives the results of the learning process. Between the input and the output layers, there exist either one or more layers that are the hidden layers. A fully connected neural network is one in which every hidden output and input are connected to each unit in layers located on either side. The connection of one unit to another is represented by a number known as a *weight*. The value of the weight can be positive or negative. A higher weight will have a higher influence on the network.

The common design of a neural network in which inputs are fed into the input layer and outputs received at the output layer is referred to as a *feedforward network*. Each unit has to receive inputs from units located to its left, then multiply by the value of the weight they have travelled along. Each unit will add all the connections it receives and, if this sum exceeds a particular threshold value, then it will fire and propagate or trigger the units it is connected to on the right side of the network.

For a neural network to learn there must be feedback. The purpose of feedback is to make a comparison between what has happened and what was expected to happen. A difference between the two is determined and one decides on how to improve next time.

Neural networks learn in the same way. The feedback process in neural networks is known as *backpropagation*. The output of the network is compared with what the network was expected to produce and this difference is used for the purpose of modifying the weights of connections between the network units. This is done from the output units to the hidden units and, lastly, to the input units. In other words, this is done while moving backwards. This process causes the neural network to learn, thus reducing the amount of the difference, normally referred to as the *network error*, between the outputs and what was targeted. The goal is to match the outputs from the network and the targeted output, but this may be difficult. An error of zero is the best, which is an indication that the artificial neural network has no error; however, achieving this can be difficult.

After using several examples to train the artificial neural network, time will be reached at which you will be in a position to give the network a new set of input data that it has not seen before and observe the output.

When to use Artificial Neural Networks

Neural networks should be used in problems that involve finding trends in data. They are good at solving problems, which humans are good at. Examples of such problems include making generalizations, image recognition, and others. They help in solving problems that are difficult or impossible to solve by use of traditional, formal analysis.

Fuzzy logic has been integrated into neural networks. This type of logic recognizes more than just the simple true/false values and provides a better simulation of the real world. Suppose you have the statement: it is sunny today. This statement can be 100% true if there are no clouds during the day, 50% in case it is hazy, 80% if there are only a few clouds, and 0% if it is rainy. This means that the concept takes into account factors like somewhat, usually, and sometimes.

A combination of fuzzy logic and neural networks has been used in application screening for jobs, automotive engineering, monitoring of glaucoma, crane control, etc. Neural networks are very good for processing huge amounts of data, which makes them very useful in image compression. More websites on the internet are using images and neural networks can help compress such images.

8-Machine Learning

Machine learning in computing is borrowed from human behavior. It is a branch of artificial intelligence that involves the design and development of systems capable of showing an improvement in performance based on their previous experiences. This means that when reacting to the same situation, a machine should show improvement from one time to the next. With machine learning, software systems are able to predict accurately without having to be programmed explicitly. The goal of machine learning is to build algorithms that can receive input data then use statistical analysis so as to predict the output value within an acceptable range.

Machine learning originated from pattern recognition and the theory that computers are able to learn without the need for programming them. Researchers in the field of artificial intelligence wanted to determine whether computers are able to learn from data. Machine learning is an iterative approach and this is why models are able to adapt as they are being exposed to new data. Models learn from their previous computations so as to give repeatable, reliable results and decisions.

The increasing popularity of machine learning can be attributed to the same reasons that have led to an increase in the popularity of data mining. Such factors include the availability of cheaper and powerful computational processing, availability of varieties of data, and affordable means for data storage. These factors make it easy for one to quickly produce models capable of analyzing bigger and more complex data in order to deliver faster and more accurate results. When an organization or business builds precise models, it becomes easy for it to identify profitable opportunities or avoid risks. With machine learning, businesses can also draw conclusions and identify patterns which can help them create models for making predictions. This can help them to make wise business decisions.

Categories of Machine Learning

Let us discuss the three categories of machine learning, namely, supervised, unsupervised, and reinforcement learning:

Supervised Learning

In supervised learning algorithms, there is a clear distinction between the explanatory and the distinction variables. The model has to be trained so as to explain the dependent variables based on the explanatory variables. This means that the output variables for the model are known beforehand. These are applicable in prediction, classification, and time-series forecasting.

The data scientist is expected to provide both the inputs and the outputs that are desired and furnish feedback based on the accuracy of the predictions during training. After completion of the training, the algorithm will have to apply what was applied to the next data.

The concept of supervised learning can be seen to be similar to human learning under a teacher's supervision. The teacher gives some examples to the student and the student then derives new rules and knowledge from these examples so as to apply this somewhere else.

It is also good for you to know the difference between regression and classification problems. In regression problems, the target is a numeric value, whereas in classification the target is a class or a tag. A regression task can help determine the average cost of all houses in London, whereas a classification task will help determine the types of flowers based on the length of their sepals and petals.

Unsupervised Learning

For the case of unsupervised learning, the output variables are unknown or the targets are not provided. There exists no distinction between the explanatory and the dependent variables. The models are usually created so as to help find the intrinsic data structure.

For the case of unsupervised learning, the algorithms do not expect to be provided with the output data. An approach called "deep learning," which is an iterative approach is used so as to review the data and arrive at new conclusions. This makes them more suitable than supervised learning algorithms for use in processing tasks that are complex. This means that the unsupervised learning algorithms learn solely from examples without responses to these. The algorithm finds patterns from the examples on its own.

Supervised learning algorithms work similarly to how humans determine any similarities between two or more objects. The majority of recommender systems you encounter when purchasing items online are based on unsupervised learning algorithms. In this case, the algorithm derives what to suggest you purchase based on what you have purchased before. The algorithm has to estimate the kind of customers whom you resemble and a suggestion is drawn from that.

Reinforcement Learning

This type of learning occurs when the algorithm is presented with examples that lack labels as is the case with unsupervised learning. However, the example can be accompanied by positive or negative feedback depending on the solution proposed by the algorithm. It is associated with applications in which the algorithm has to make decisions and each decision is associated with a consequence, similar to trial-and-error in human learning.

Errors become useful in learning when they are associated with a penalty such as pain, cost, loss of time, etc. In reinforced learning, some actions are more likely to succeed compared with others.

Machine learning processes are similar to those of data mining and predictive modeling. In both cases, searching through the data is required so as to draw patterns and then adjust the actions of the program accordingly. A good example of machine learning is the recommender systems. If you purchase an item online, then you will see ads related to that item: that is a good example of machine learning.

Common Machine Learning Frameworks

When venturing into machine learning, it may be hard for you to choose a framework from the many that are available. You may be aware of the many machine learning frameworks, but it is good to weigh the alternatives in terms of speed, scalability, and ease of use. Let us discuss the various machine learning frameworks.

Brainstorm

Brainstorm is one of the easiest machine learning frameworks for one to master based on its flexibility and simplicity. If you need to create a neural network machine learning model, then Brainstorm is the best framework for you. It makes learning faster and fun. Brainstorm is written in Python and was developed to run smoothly on backend systems.

The framework provides two data APIs, or data handlers, using Python. One for these is for leveraging GPUs using CUDA while the other one is for CPUs using Numpy library.

Apache Singa

Apache Singa is a machine learning framework good for distributed deep learning. Apache Singa works by partitioning the model and parallelizing the process of model training. The user is provided with a robust and simple machine learning model capable of working across a cluster of nodes. The framework is highly applied in natural language processing (NLP) and image recognition.

The framework is very flexible, making it capable of running synchronous, asynchronous, and hybrid training models, giving it the capability to support a wide variety of deep learning models. The model comprises three important parts, including the IO, the model, and the core. The IO part has the classes necessary for reading and writing data to and from disks and networks. The core is responsible for memory management and tensor operations while the model contains the data structures and algorithms responsible for machine learning. The Apache Singa framework scales very well to cater to large training datasets.

Caffe

Caffe is a machine learning framework that provides better speed, expression, and modularity. The framework was developed with these as the focus. The framework is widely used in image classification/computer vision and it works by leveraging Convolutional Neural Networks (CNNs). Its Model Zoo, which is a set of models that have been trained, makes it popular. One is not expected to write any code to use these models.

Note that Caffe is only applicable in computer vision. If you need to build a model to work with text, then this is not the best model for you. Caffe can be used on a wide variety of hardware and one can switch between GPU and CPU by use of a single flag.

Theano

Most people know Theano as a low-end machine learning framework, but it provides high flexibility. The framework is also fast in doing machine learning tasks. Theano shows cryptic error messages when running. If you are doing a research task, then this is the best platform for you.

Amazon Machine Learning

The AML is a machine learning service developed by Amazon for use by developers. It contains several tools that can be used for developing high-end, sophisticated, and intelligent learning models without writing any code. The tool also provides various APIs for making predictions needed for the applications. This service is very flexible and highly used by Amazon's data scientists to power their Amazon Cloud Services. It can be connected to data stored in Amazon S3, Redshift, or RDS for performing tasks such as regression, binary classification, or multi-class categorization so as to create some new models.

Accord.NET

This is an open-source machine learning framework based on .NET. It is ideal for use in scientific computing. It has a number of libraries applicable in pattern recognition, statistical data processing, artificial neural networks, image processing, linear algebra, and others. The libraries for the framework come in the form of source code, installers, and NuGet packages. It also comes with a matrix library that can be used for facilitating algorithmic changes and code reusability.

Apache Mahout

This is an open-source software developed by the Apache Software Foundation for the purpose of providing a scalable or distributed machine learning framework to be applied in classification, clustering, and collaborative filtering. Mahout also has Java collections for various Java libraries and computational operations. It has been deployed on top of Hadoop by using the MapReduce paradigm. It is highly applicable where one needs to get insight into data. After connecting the Big Data stored in Hadoop, this tool can help you to identify some useful patterns in the data.

The Apache Software Foundation uses Mahout to implement its distributed learning models.

9-Data Collection, Modelling, and Compilation

Data Collection

Data scientists usually find it difficult to find a relevant dataset to their work. The majority of organization databases are filled with both relevant and irrelevant datasets. This means that data scientists have to move from one department to another or contact different departments in order to collect relevant data. In some cases, they have to wait for weeks.

After receiving the data, the data scientist will spend time exploring the data and trying to draw meaningful insights. For example, the data may not be presented in a format that is easy to understand or they may not understand the meaning of some of the fields in the tables. They could have access to little or no metadata to help them, meaning that they have to look for help from the owners of the data so as to be able to understand it.

There are various methods that one can use for data collection. One has to request and obtain pertinent data from the necessary organizations or individuals through the appropriate means. The respondent can provide the data directly or through an interview. There might also be a need to extract data from administrative sources. In such a case, one will have to ask for permission so as to be granted access to the administrative records

The choice of data collection method is influenced by a number of factors. Such factors include the degree of accuracy required, the variable type, the strategy for data collection, and the skills of the enumerator. Common data collection methods are described below.

Observation

This gives the data collector first-hand, primary information, meaning that the collected data will be void of bias. It includes experimental, systematic field observation, and participant observation. Although it is more expensive, it is more accurate.

The data collector has to travel to the field to collect the data. S/He does not rely on any other person to collect the data but instead reports their own direct observations.

Interviewing

One can prefer structured telephone interviews or self-administered questionnaires. This is a good data collection method where the questions are complex. An interview can be carried out in any of the following ways:

1. Face-to-face interviews - in this type of interview, the interviewer will have an advantage in that he/she will be able to establish rapport with the participants and make them cooperative. This is the type of interview that yields the highest response rate in surveys and researches. In case of any ambiguous answers, the interviewer is able to seek clarification from the interviewee and seek follow-up information. However, it may not be appropriate when a high number of respondents are involved.

2. Telephone interviews - this type of interview can be conducted on any respondent who has a telephone. It is less expensive and less time-consuming. However, the interviewer will not get a higher response rate as is the case with face-to-face interviews.

Questionnaires

These are forms that are completed and returned by the respondents. It is a good data collection technique where the respondent is willing to cooperate and where there are high literacy rates.

The data collector can create two types of questions:

1. Closed questions - in this type of questions, the data collector asks questions to which the respondent is expected to give simple responses like "yes" or "no." No further explanation is required. Such types of

questionnaires are easy to analyze and takes the respondent a shorter time to complete.

2. Open-ended questions - in these types of questions, the data collector asks questions that require the respondent to give explanations. These take the respondents a longer time to complete and the data collector to analyze the responses. Some of the responses provided may be ambiguous.

Once raw data have been collected from the field, we must compile it so that we can perform taxonomic analysis on it by breaking it into its respective segments and parts. If the data are kept in different files, then it must be brought together for a proper analysis. It is after this that you will be able to analyze the data and derive information from it.

When dealing with data obtained from different sources and kept in different files, you will come across a number of challenges, including missing values, outliers, noise, etc. Let us discuss how to solve such problems during data compilation.

Cleaning and Organizing Data

Research has shown that the leading challenge to data scientists is dirty data. Many are the times you will find a data scientist cleaning, formatting, and even sampling data, a task that consumes much time. This means that when working as a data scientist, targeting clean data can help you save much time.

Data obtained from the real world always has some missing values. Data mining and machine learning models trained using data with missing values usually give inaccurate or unreliable results. This means that in data analysis, one must consider the process of handling missing values for the purpose of enhancing the accuracy of the results.

Suppose you are conducting an online survey about a certain product. In some cases, people will not share information about themselves. People will give you their experience, but not the period of time they have been using the product. Others will also opt not to share their contact information. This means that in most cases involving real-life problems, we will always some missing values. This is one of the tasks of a data scientist.

Handling Missing Data

Data obtained from the real world always has some missing values. Data mining and machine learning models trained using data with missing values usually give inaccurate or unreliable results. This means that in data science, we must consider the process of handling missing values for the purpose of enhancing the accuracy of the results.

Suppose you are conducting an online survey about a certain product. In some cases, people will not share information about themselves. People will give you their experience, but not the period of time they have been using the product. Others will also opt not to share their contact information. This means that in most cases involving real-life problems, we will always some missing values.

Some of the methods for handling missing data include the following:

- Replacing it with scalar values such as NaN.
- Fill NA Forward and Backward - for each row with NaN values, the values of the immediate row at the top or bottom are used for filling.
- Dropping - the missing values are dropped.
- Replacement - the missing value can be replaced with a specific value.

How to Avoid Dirty Data

Dirty data refers to data that contain inconsistencies and noise. Such data has a negative effect on training, validation, and the application of machine learning models. To avoid this, you should come up with mechanisms for filtering data before it is saved. Keeping duplicates of data should also be avoided as this may cause inconsistencies. Again, before you get data from sources, ask the source what they do so as to ensure that the data are clean.

Dirty data may also result from typing errors. This is why you should have someone dedicated to keying data into your systems and don't allow just anybody to do it.

Modeling/Machine Learning

After the above tasks, the data scientist has to suggest the machine learning and predictive modeling frameworks depending on the business requirements.

It is said that developing a problem is not a big problem to data scientists, but the problem lies in defining the problem and coming up with a means to measure the solution. This becomes harder when the data scientist doesn't have a clear definition of what they want. If what is delivered by the models is not related to the business requirements, then the data scientist will have to explain the source of the discrepancies and what went wrong.

In modeling, the data scientist is expected to choose a machine learning algorithm to create the model. There are different types of machine learning algorithms and these have been discussed in this book. The data may have to be split into training and test datasets. The training dataset will be used for training the model while the test set will be used for testing the model. Once the model has been created, trained, and tested it can be used for making predictions.

Refining Algorithms

There are a number of ways through which this can be done and it is a process that can run for many months before completion. This also means that the data scientist has a tough job choosing how to refine the algorithm.

Algorithms are not always described sufficiently to describe a computer algorithm. This means that there is a need for us to describe an algorithm in the best way possible. In computer algorithms, there is always a need to make some initializations before processing can begin. This means that it is good for this to be indicated, especially in the first few lines of the algorithm. Consider the steps given below that show how to describe an algorithm:

1. Carry out required initializations
2. While not reaching the file end

3. Do

4. Read in the next number

5. Add the number to the accumulated sum

6. Increment the count of the input numbers

7. End do

8. Calculate the average

Once the algorithm has been refined, it becomes easy to understand and use for data analysis.

Building Training Sets

Datasets form the essential unit on which data scientists relies. In some cases, the data scientist is required to do scaling, decomposition, and aggregation transformations on the data before training the models.

The purpose of a training dataset is to train the algorithm to learn using concepts like neural networks. It comprises both the input data and the expected result.

The majority (not less than 60%) of your data should be used as the training set. In most cases, 80% of the data are used as the training dataset. This is because if the model is not trained well, it will give poor results and poor training can lead to overfitting or underfitting.

Overfitting occurs when the model is too detailed such that noise and outliers in the data are treated as patterns. Underfitting is when the model is too simple such that it cannot extract the underlying patterns from the data. If you use a small amount of data for training your model, then your model will most likely experience the problem of underfitting. That is why you have to assign an adequate amount of data for training your model.

As you know, data science is a combination of disciplines such as mathematics, statistics, business use cases, communication skills, and programming; hence, the tasks of a data scientist are not about data handling alone. This means that a data scientist will have to perform other tasks including the following:

- Create open-ended industry questions and do undirected research.
- Examine and explore the data from different angles so as to identify the hidden trends, weaknesses, and opportunities.
- Report predictions and findings to the necessary authorities, such as management, using necessary tools such as reports and visualizations.
- Recommend any cost-effective changes to the current strategies and procedures.

After compiling and modeling the data, it is then prepared for analysis. The following are some of the practices involved in data preparation.

Dealing with Outliers

An outlier is simply an observation that appears at an abnormal distance from the other values of a random sample obtained from a given population. When dealing with data, most people forget the outliers. Even in controlled experiments, outliers are a common occurrence. They are normally caused by errors in measurements or by faulty measuring or recording instruments.

The best way for you to detect outliers in your data is to use graphical means. However, it is possible for you to detect outliers by using statistical methods and tools such as R, Python, Excel, etc. Scatter plots and box plots are two common ways of detecting outliers. A histogram can also help you detect outliers in your data.

There are many strategies that can be used to deal with outliers and most tools used for detecting outliers also provide the means for dealing with them, although they differ in how this is done.

Let us discuss some useful strategies for handling outliers.

Create a Filter in the Testing Tool

Suppose you have an A/B testing tool that you use to track revenue. You can create a code to help filter out abnormally large orders from the test results. Past analytics data can help you determine the average web order and the filter should be created with this in consideration. If you find the average to be $100, then any order above $150 can be considered to be an outlier.

Change or Remove Outliers during the Post-test Analysis

One can choose to remove the outliers or trim the dataset so as to exclude as many outliers as possible. Trimming of values is easy in Excel by use of the TRIMMEAN function. You only specify the array to be manipulated and the amount by which you need to trim the upper and the lower extremities.

Trimming values is also easy in R by use of the mean function. If the mean and the median differ so much, then this is an indication that there are either large or small values that skew it. To solve this, you can trim a certain percentage of data on both the large and small sides. You can use mean(x, trim = .05), in which x will be the dataset, but you can choose the value you need to replace the .05.

Changing the Outlier Value

In this method, instead of removing the outlier, you can take it and give it another value that represents your data more sensibly. This way, you will have discarded the extreme values. However, you might experience a challenge in determining the value with which you replace the outlier. There are various methods to do this. Instead of using the more technical and complex processes to determine this, you can identify the value in your data, which makes sense, and use it for replacement. This way, you will have standard data for training your model.

Box – Cox Transformation

This involves the transformation of the data until it is normally distributed. There are a number of transformations that can make your transformed data normal. A good example is squaring the data values as this can give you normal values. You can also find the reciprocal or the square root of the data and this can give you normal values. In some other cases, the logarithms for the data values can be distributed normally. All the transformations that give normally distributed data can be grouped together into a Box–Cox transformation. The Box–Cox transformation takes the following formula:

$$y = x^\lambda \; for \; \lambda \neq 0 \; and \; y = \ln(x) \; for \; \lambda = 0$$

In this case, x is the raw data, y represents the transformed data, and lambda represents the transformation constant. If lambda is given a value of 1, then no transformation will be done. If the value of lambda is 2, then it represents a squared transformation function.

There are a number of ways through which you can find the value of lambda in the Box–Cox transformation. One of those ways is the Most Likely Estimate (MLE) approach. However, this can be a long process. The easiest way for you to find the value of lambda is by varying its value between −5 and 5. Then, it is your duty to determine the value of lambda that will give you a distribution close to a normal distribution. The best value of lambda is the one with the smallest standard deviation of the variation between transformed and normally distributed data. This will help you resolve the skewness of your data.

Winsorize (Threshold Control)

In this method, the outliers are replaced with the largest value in the data that is not considered to be an outlier. The process of replacing the extreme values is known as *winsorization*. In most cases, winsorization involves setting all the extreme outliers to some specified percentile of your data. If you are using a winsorization of 90%, for example, all the data below the 5th percentile will be set to the 5th percentile while all data above the 95th percentile will be set to the 95th percentile. The winsorized estimators are known to be more robust to the outliers compared with more standard forms. The purpose of winsorizing the outliers is to bring them down to some specified value closer to a normal distribution curve.

All the outliers can be brought down to the value you calculate, but others will prefer to bring the lowest outlier to that value and bring the next one down to it, bring the next one down to it but add something little to it, and so it continues. This way, the values will be corrected, but they will remain in the same order, from the lowest to the highest. The value to be added can be chosen by determining the scale of the variable you need to correct. However, it is good for you to note that if the addition is small, there is a high probability that there will be no change to the statistical output.

Once you deal with the outliers, there will be a higher chance to get the right result at the end. The amount by which an outlier affects your analysis depends on a number of factors including the size of the dataset. If the dataset is large, then each observation will be carrying less weight, meaning that the effect of an outlier will be minimal. This is not the case with a small dataset where each observation carries huge weight. However, with the above three ways, you will take care of outliers and perform the right analysis.

Reindexing

The purpose of reindexing is to change the column and row labels of the data. Reindexing means conforming data to match a certain set of labels along a given axis. There are various operations that we can accomplish through the process of reindexing. Examples include reordering existing data to match a set of new labels and inserting NA (missing values) markers to label locations in which the label has no existing data.

The purpose of indexing is to make data easily accessible. The impact of this will be improved performance. Suppose you have some data in a database. If a change is made to the data stored in that database, then it needs to be reindexed to ensure that access to the data is still easy. A good example is when the price of an item is changed from $5.99 to $4.99. In such a case, the price change must be reindexed. It will then become easy to access the value of the new price for the item.

10-Data Analysis

Data analysis involves processing data in order to discover hidden patterns, trends, and relationships between the data variables. Such patterns, trends, and relationships can be used for decision making. The analysis is done using statistical and analytical tools.

Data Analysis Methods

There are various methods that can be used for data analysis. Let us discuss them.

Data Mining

This is a data analysis method used for finding patterns in large datasets using the methods of artificial intelligence, statistics, machine learning, and databases. The goal of data mining is to transform raw data into business information that is understandable. This may involve identifying groups in data records/cluster analysis or identifying dependencies and anomalies between data groups.

Data mining is highly applied in anomaly detection where outliers are identified and eliminated from decision making. It is also applied in determining customer purchasing habits, which can also be used for decision making.

Text Analytics

Text analytics is a process used to derive useful information from text. It involves the processing of unstructured textual information, extracting useful numerical indices from the information, and making the information available to machine learning and statistical algorithms for further processing.

Text analytics involves any or all of the steps given below:

- Collection of information from various sources such as file system, web, etc.
- Linguistic analysis such as natural language processing.
- Pattern recognition such as recognition of email addresses, phone numbers etc.
- Extraction of summary information from text like relative frequencies of words, identifying similarities between sets of documents, etc.

Text analytics is applied in processing open-ended survey questions, analyzing log files for intrusion detection in security systems, analysis of emails to detect spam emails, etc.

Business Intelligence

Business intelligence refers to the transformation of data into actionable intelligence for business purposes, which may be good for strategic and tactical decision making in business. With business intelligence, individuals are provided with a way to derive insights from their collected data by observing the data trends.

Today, business intelligence is applied in budgeting and rolling forecasts, making operating decisions in businesses such as pricing and product placement, assessing the demand of products in different market segments, etc.

Data Analysis Process

Quality data analysis is of the essence. Once you have the data, you need to know whether:

- it is the right data to answer the questions that you have.
- you can draw accurate and meaningful conclusions from the data.
- the data is good for decision making in your business.

If you use the right tools and processes for decision making, then you will be able to draw the right conclusions from your data. The following steps will help you accomplish data analysis successfully.

Define your Questions

In any business or organization data analysis, one has to begin with the right questions. The questions should be clear, measurable, and concise. You should design the questions in such a way that they either qualify or disqualify the potential solutions to your specific opportunity or problem.

For example, you can begin with a clearly defined problem, like the company contract has been experiencing rising costs and cannot submit competitive contract proposals. One of the questions that can help in solving this business problem includes: is it possible for the company to reduce the number of staff members without negatively affecting the quality?

Create Clear Measurement Priorities

This can be done in the following two steps:

- Know what to measure

What data do you need so as to answer your question? In the example of the government contractor, you should know the total number as well as the cost of the current staff. You also need to get the percentage of time that they spend in doing important business functions. To answer such a question, you will probably have to answer numerous sub-questions such as are the current staff members under-utilized? If yes, what process improvements can be done? Also, ensure that you include any objections that may arise from the stakeholders.

- Know how to measure it

It will be important for you to know how to measure data, especially before you collect it because your measuring process can either back up or discredit your later analysis. Some of the questions that you need to ask yourself include:

- What is the available timeframe? For example, annual vs. quarterly costs.

- What unit of measure will be used? For example, EUR vs. USD.

- What are the factors that should be included? For example, only staff salary vs. staff salary vs. annual benefits for the staff.

Analyze Data

At this point, the assumption is that you have already collected data. It is now time for you to perform a deep analysis of the data so that you may answer your question. First, Thuis use different ways to modify your data, for example, creating excel pivot tables, creating plots, and finding correlations.

With a pivot table, you will be able to use various variables to filter the data. It also allows you to calculate the mean, minimum, maximum, and the standard deviation of your data.

During data manipulation, you may realize that you have the perfect data, but you may have to collect more data or reframe your question. In all cases, this initial process of data analysis will help you focus on answering your question and dealing with any possible objections.

This is also the step in which you use data analysis software tools such as Weka, Minitab, Stata, etc. Other than software tools, you may prefer to use programming languages such as R and Python.

Interpret Results

Now that you have analyzed your data and conducted further research, it is time for you to interpret the results. During this step, you cannot prove a hypothesis as true, but you can fail to reject it. If your interpretation answers the question, then you will end up with a meaningful conclusion.

11-Data Presentation and Visualization

Data presentation involves the use of pictorials such as maps, graphs, charts, and other methods to present the data to users. With such mechanisms, a visual aspect can be added to data that makes it easy to understand.

The way you present data to users matters a lot. It can be a deal maker or a deal breaker.

Types of Data Presentation

The presentation method may impress or fail to impress the decision makers. Let us discuss the various methods used in data science for data presentation.

Frequency Distribution

This is a table that shows how often every value of a variable in question occurs in the dataset. We can use a frequency distribution table to summarize categorical or numerical data. The frequencies are also represented in the form of relative frequencies, that is, the percentage of the total number in a sample.

The following is an example of a frequency distribution table:

Class	Class 1	Percentage
No. of Males	32	55.17%
No. of Females	26	44.83%
Total	58	

Graphical Methods

We can illustrate frequency distributions by plotting different types of graphs. The type of graph to use is determined by a number of factors including the type of data, the amount of data, and even personal choice. The different types of graphs that you can plot include bar graphs, line graphs, histograms, pie charts, etc.

Data Visualization in Python

The Python programming language provides its users with various libraries that they can use for data visualization. However, if you need to get a plot quickly, then matplotlib is the best library to use. It forms the foundation for several other plotting libraries such as Pandas.

Matplotlib

This library should be installed. If you have already installed Python on your system, then you can use pip3 to install matplotlib. You just have to run the following command:

```
pip3 install matplotlib
```

```
C:\Users\admin>pip3 install matplotlib
Collecting matplotlib
  Downloading https://files.pythonhosted.org/packages/ce/02/d0fb7dc284a56449f782
5ef7d1e8b682bf44cef540a6d615e1fa0faa543a/matplotlib-2.2.2-cp35-cp35m-win_amd64.w
hl (8.7MB)
    100% |################################| 8.7MB 254kB/s
Collecting cycler>=0.10 (from matplotlib)
  Downloading https://files.pythonhosted.org/packages/f7/d2/e07d3ebb2bd7af696440
ce7e754c59dd546ffe1bbe732c8ab68b9c834e61/cycler-0.10.0-py2.py3-none-any.whl
Requirement already satisfied: python-dateutil>=2.1 in c:\users\admin\appdata\lo
cal\programs\python\python35\lib\site-packages (from matplotlib) (2.6.1)
Collecting kiwisolver>=1.0.1 (from matplotlib)
  Downloading https://files.pythonhosted.org/packages/67/57/834881c80cd1361792a1
8b67ac8c1638c224a484956582e51d2f9e16e30/kiwisolver-1.0.1-cp35-none-win_amd64.wh
l (57kB)
    100% |################################| 61kB 75kB/s
Requirement already satisfied: numpy>=1.7.1 in c:\users\admin\appdata\local\prog
rams\python\python35\lib\site-packages (from matplotlib) (1.13.3)
Requirement already satisfied: pytz in c:\users\admin\appdata\local\programs\pyt
hon\python35\lib\site-packages (from matplotlib) (2017.2)
Requirement already satisfied: six>=1.10 in c:\users\admin\appdata\local\program
s\python\python35\lib\site-packages (from matplotlib) (1.11.0)
Collecting pyparsing!=2.0.4,!=2.1.2,!=2.1.6,>=2.0.1 (from matplotlib)
  Downloading https://files.pythonhosted.org/packages/6a/8a/718fd7d3458f9fab8e67
186b00abdd345b639976bc7fb3ae722e1b026a50/pyparsing-2.2.0-py2.py3-none-any.whl (5
6kB)
    100% |################################| 61kB 77kB/s
Requirement already satisfied: setuptools in c:\users\admin\appdata\local\progra
ms\python\python35\lib\site-packages (from kiwisolver>=1.0.1->matplotlib) (18.2)

Installing collected packages: cycler, kiwisolver, pyparsing, matplotlib
Successfully installed cycler-0.10.0 kiwisolver-1.0.1 matplotlib-2.2.2 pyparsing
-2.2.0

C:\Users\admin>
```

Matplotlib has a context on which one or more plots may be drawn before saving or showing the image on a file. The context is accessible via functions on *pyplot*. There is a convention through which you can import matplotlib as *plt*.

This is shown below:

```
import matplotlib.pyplot as plt
```

To create plots and charts, we call on context as follows:

```
pyplot.plot(...)
```

Elements like labels, axis, legends, and others can be accessed and configured on the context in the form of separate function calls.

The drawings on context may be shown in a new window after calling the *show()* function. This is illustrated below:

```
# show the plot
pyplot.show()
```

It is also possible to save the drawings on the context to a file like a PNG-formatted file. To save images, call the *savefig()* function. This is shown below:

```
pyplot.savefig('image.png')
```

Line Plot

This is a good way to represent observations made at regular intervals. On the *x*-axis, a regular interval like time is shown. The observations are shown on the *y*-axis ordered by an *x*-axis and a line is used to connect them.

To create a line, we call the *plot()* function then pass data for the *x*-axis for the regular interval and *y*-axis for the observations:

```
# generating a line plot
```

```
pyplot.plot(x, y)
```

Line plots are good for presenting time-series data and any sequence data in which the observations are ordered. Consider the following example:

```
# Generating a line plot
from numpy import sin
from matplotlib import pyplot
# A consistent interval for the x-axis
a = [a*0.1 for a in range(50)]
# function of a for the y-axis
b = sin(a)
# Generate the line plot
pyplot.plot(a, b)
# display line plot
pyplot.show()
```

What we have done is created a sequence of 50 floating point values for the *x*-axis and a sine wave function for *x*-axis as the *y*-axis. The code gives the line plot given below:

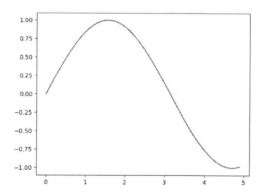

B a r   C h a r t

This type of chart is used when there is a need to present relative quantities for numerous categories. The categories are presented on the *x*-axis and they are spaced evenly. The quantity for each category is shown on the *y*-axis and is drawn as a bar starting from the baseline to the correct level on the *y*-axis.

To create a bar chart, we call the *bar()* function and pass the names of the categories on the *x*-axis and *y*-axis on the *y*-axis:

```
# Generate a bar chart
pyplot.bar(x, y)
```

Bars are very good when comparing multiple estimations or point quantities. For example:

```
# creating a bar chart
from random import seed
from random import randint
from matplotlib import pyplot
# seed a random number generator
seed(1)
# category names
x = ['Prado', 'Harrier', 'Mark X']
# quantities sold for each category
y = [randint(0, 100), randint(0, 100), randint(0,
100)]
# generate the bar chart
pyplot.bar(x, y)
# display the line plot
pyplot.show()
```

We have created three categories: Prado, Harrier, and Mark X. A single random integer has been drawn to represent the value of each category.

The code generated the bar chart shown below.

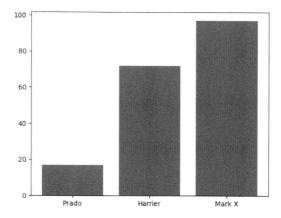

Histogram

This tool is used for summarizing the distribution of data. The *x*-axis shows the intervals for observations or discrete bins. If you have observations whose values range between 1 and 20, for example, then they can be split into 10 bins. The first bin will have [1,2], the second bin will have [3,4], and this continues.

The count or the frequency of the observations is shown on the *y*-axis. To create a histogram, we call the *hist()* function. The list or the array with the data to be represented in the histogram are passed as the argument:

```
# Generate a histogram plot
pyplot.hist(a)
```

Consider the following example:

```
# Generating a histogram plot
from numpy.random import seed
from numpy.random import randn
from matplotlib import pyplot
# seed a random number generator
seed(1)
# To get random numbers from Gaussian distribution
a = randn(300)
```

```
# Generate histogram plot
pyplot.hist(a)
# show line plot
pyplot.show()
```

In the above example, we have created a dataset of 300 random numbers that have been drawn from a Gaussian distribution. The dataset is then plotted to generate the following histogram.

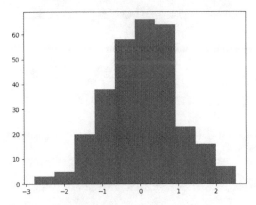

It is recommended that one should be kept when choosing the number of bins. This way, it will be easy for them to tell the shape of the distribution of the data. To specify the number of bins, you should use the *bins* argument as shown below:

```
# Generate a histogram plot
pyplot.hist(a, bins=100)
```

Box and Whisker Plot

This tool is used for illustrating how a data sample is distributed. The x-axis represents the data sample and we can draw multiple box plots side-by-side on the x-axis if needed.

The values for the observations are shown on the y-axis. A box is drawn summarizing the middle 50% of the dataset

---

beginning with the observation at the 25th percentile and ending at the 75th percentile. The 50th percentile, which is the median, is drawn using a line. The difference between the 75th and 25th percentiles is multiplied by 1.5 to give a line known as the *interquartile range*. Lines, called "whiskers," are also drawn to extend both ends of the box of the length of IQR to show the range of the sensible values for the distribution. Observations that are outside the whiskers are known as outliers and are drawn using small circles.

To draw box plots in matplotlib, we call the *boxplot()* function. The data to be represented in the box plot are passed as an argument to the function. It can be used as follows:

```
# Generating a box and whisker plot
pyplot.boxplot(a)
```

Box plots are an alternative to histograms for summarizing the distribution of data. Example:

```
# Creating a box and whisker plot
from numpy.random import seed
from numpy.random import randn
from matplotlib import pyplot
# seed a random number generator
seed(1)
# random numbers obtained from Gaussian distribution
a = [randn(300), 5 * randn(300), 10 * randn(300)]
# generate the box and whisker plot
pyplot.boxplot(a)
# display line plot
pyplot.show()
```

In the above example, we are creating three box plots in a single chart. Each of these summarizes a data sample that has been obtained from different Gaussian distributions. Each data sample is created in the form of an array and the three arrays are added into a list that in turn is passed to a plotting function. The code generates the following once executed.

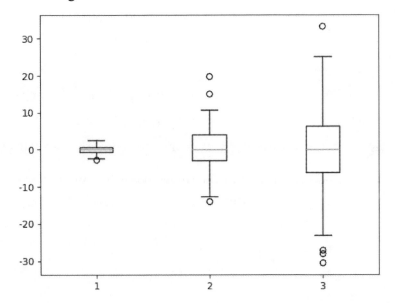

The chart has three box and whisker plots. A similar scale has been used for the y-axis. The black box represents the middle of the data, which is 50%. The orange line represents the median while the box and whisker lines give a summary of the sensible data. The dots show any outliers in your data.

Scatter Plot

This diagram is used to show the relationship between two data samples that are paired. By paired we mean that a single observation has two recordings, like the height and weight of an individual. The values of observation for the first sample are recorded on the x-axis and the values for the second sample on the y-axis. On the plot, every single point represents a single observation.

To create scatter plots with matplotlib, we call the *scatter()* function. The arrays for the two data samples are then passed into the function as the arguments. This is shown below:

```
# generate a scatter plot
pyplot.scatter(x, y)
```

Scatter plots are very good for showing how two variables are correlated. We can quantify a relationship, like drawing the line of best fit.

It may happen that observation has more than two measures. This can be represented visually by use of a scatter plot matrix. Consider the example given below:

```
# Creating a scatter plot
from numpy.random import seed
from numpy.random import randn
from matplotlib import pyplot
# seed a random number generator
seed(1)
# create the first variable
a = 20 * randn(300) + 100
# create the second variable
b = a + (10 * randn(300) + 50)
# generate a scatter plot
pyplot.scatter(a, b)
# display line plot
pyplot.show()
```

We began by creating two related data samples. The first sample was generated from a Gaussian distribution. The second sample relies on the first sample and is obtained by adding the second random Gaussian value to the value of the first measure. The code generates the following once executed:

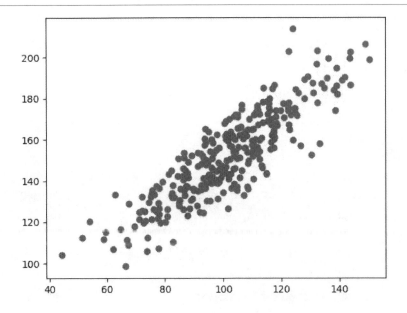

Data Visualization in R

R is a programming language and one of the best tools available in data science. R has various ways through which you can present your data visually. R also has a set of inbuilt libraries and functions that can be used for presenting data visually.

Before getting started, ensure that you have installed R studio into your system. After that, you should ensure that you have installed all the packages that enable data visualization. The package simply helps you extend the functionalities offered by R. You should install the following packages:

- tidyverse packages - this is a collection of packages for R that rely on the same programming philosophy. They include the following:

  - readr - this helps in importing data into R.

- dplyr - this is good for data manipulation.

- ggpubr and ggplot2 - good for data visualization. The ggpubr package helps one create publication-ready plots easily.

Once you install the tidyverse package, you will have installed packages like ggplot, readr, dplyr, and others. To install the tidyverse package, run the following command on the R console:

```
install.packages("tidyverse")
```

```
> install.packages("tidyverse")
Warning in install.packages("tidyverse") :
  'lib = "C:/Program Files/R/R-3.6.1/library"' is not writable
--- Please select a CRAN mirror for use in this session ---
also installing the dependencies 'colorspace', 'sys', 'ps', 'highr', 'markdown'$

trying URL 'https://cloud.r-project.org/bin/windows/contrib/3.6/colorspace_1.4-$
Content type 'application/zip' length 2550133 bytes (2.4 MB)
downloaded 2.4 MB

trying URL 'https://cloud.r-project.org/bin/windows/contrib/3.6/sys_3.2.zip'
Content type 'application/zip' length 59750 bytes (58 KB)
downloaded 58 KB
```

The installation may take several minutes, so be patient.

After that, you should install the latest version of ggpubr package. This can be installed by running this command:

```
if(!require(devtools)) install.packages("devtools")
devtools::install_github("kassambara/ggpubr")
```

If the above command doesn't work, then use this command to install the ggpubr package:

```
install.packages("ggpubr")
```

Once the packages have been installed, run the following commands on the terminal to load them into your workspace:

```
library("ggplot2")
library("ggpubr")
```

Now that the packages have been loaded into the workspace, we can call functions like *ggscatter*() to help create a scatter plot for data. If you need to know how a particular function is used, type it on the R console while preceding it with a question mark (?). For example, to know how to use the *ggscatter* function, type the following on R console:

```
?ggscatter
```

The data about the usage of the function will be opened in your default browser.

Data Format

It is expected that your data should be presented in a rectangular format, in which the columns are the variables while the rows are the observations. The names of the columns should adhere to the naming conventions of R. Columns with special characters and blank space should be avoided. The column names should not begin with a number, but only a letter or an underscore (_). Any missing value in the data should be replaced with N/A (Not Applicable).

Importing Data

You should first save the data in a csv or text file. The following code can help you import the data into R. Note that we are using the *readr* library to import the data:

```
library("readr")
# Reads files delimited by tab   (.txt tab)
data<- read_tsv(file.choose())
# Reads files delimited by comma (,)   (.csv)
data <- read_csv(file.choose())
# Reads semicolon(;) separated files(.csv)
data <- read_csv2(file.choose())
```

R comes with a number of datasets that can be used for demonstration purposes. Examples of such data include mtacars, Longley, iris, etc. Whenever you need to load a dataset, just call the *data()* function and pass the name of the dataset as the argument. The function *head* will help you inspect the data. To get the first four rows of the mtcars dataset, we run the following code:

```
data("mtcars") # Loading
head(mtcars, n=5) # Print the first n = 5 rows
```

```
> data("mtcars") # Loading
> head(mtcars, n=5) # Print the first n = 5 rows
                   mpg cyl disp  hp drat    wt  qsec vs am gear carb
Mazda RX4         21.0   6  160 110 3.90 2.620 16.46  0  1    4    4
Mazda RX4 Wag     21.0   6  160 110 3.90 2.875 17.02  0  1    4    4
Datsun 710        22.8   4  108  93 3.85 2.320 18.61  1  1    4    1
Hornet 4 Drive    21.4   6  258 110 3.08 3.215 19.44  1  0    3    1
Hornet Sportabout 18.7   8  360 175 3.15 3.440 17.02  0  0    3    2
> |
```

The first five rows of the dataset have been printed. If you need to get the details of the dataset, then type the following:

```
?mtcars
```

R comes with different functions that can be used for drawing different types of graphs and charts.

Scatter Plot

A scatter plot helps to show the relationship between two continuous variables. Let us create a scatter plot from the iris dataset:

```
plot( x = iris$Sepal.Length, y = iris$Sepal.Width,
pch = 20, cex = 0.9, frame = FALSE, xlab = "Sepal
Length",ylab = "Sepal Width")
```

When executed on the R console, the above code will return the following:

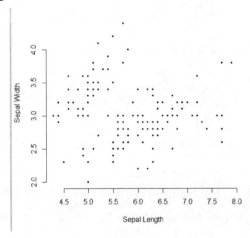

It is possible for us to load our own dataset and draw a scatter plot from it. In my case, I am loading the dataset with two columns. The data show the relationship between hours of study and the marks scored. After loading the data, I can draw a scatter plot to show the relationship between *hours* and *marks*.

```
library("readr")
# Reads files delimited by tab  (.txt tab)
```

```
mydata<- read_tsv(file.choose())
plot(  x = mydata$Hours, y = mydata$Marks, pch = 20,
cex = 0.9, frame = FALSE,   xlab = "Hours",ylab =
"Marks")
```

The code returns the following scatter plot:

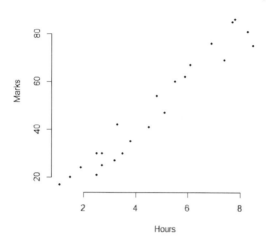

B o x   P l o t

A box plot is used in plotting a combination of continuous and

categorical variables. It is a good tool for you to show how data are

spread and for detecting outliers. It will show you the five

important numbers for your data: the minimum, 25th percentile,

median, 75th percentile, and the maximum. To create a box plot in

R, we have to call the boxplot function as shown below:

```
boxplot(Sepal.Length ~ Species, data = iris, ylab =
"Sepal.Length",           frame = FALSE, col =
"lightgray")
```

This returns the following box plot:

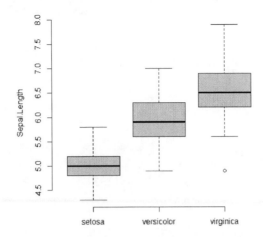

The box plot has been created from the iris dataset that comes with R. We can also build a box plot from the data that we have loaded ourselves. This is shown below:

```
library("readr")
# Reads files delimited by tab  (.txt tab)
mydata<- read_tsv(file.choose())
boxplot(Hours ~ Marks, data = mydata, ylab = "Marks",
frame = FALSE, col = "lightgray"
```
The code returns the following box plot:

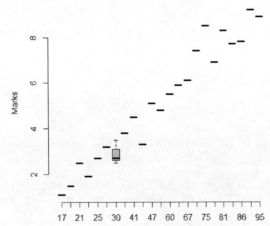

If there are outliers in your data, then they are shown at the top in the form of dots.

Histogram

A histogram helps us plot a continuous variable. The data are broken into a number of bins and the distribution of bins is shown. The size of the bin can be changed at any time to observe the effect it has on the visualization. The *ggplot2* package is the best for creating a histogram. We use the *geom_histogram()* method to draw the histogram. The *bins* option will help you control the number of bars in the histogram and the *binwidth* can help you control the amount of width that will be covered by each bar. However, when dealing with continuous variables, it is recommended that we use the *geom_histogram()* method as it will allow us to control both the width and the number of bins.

In this section, we will use the mpg dataset to draw a histogram. This dataset comes in-built in R and shows the details of various cars. To see this, type *mpg* on the R console:

```
> mpg
# A tibble: 234 x 11
   manufacturer model    displ  year   cyl trans    drv     cty   hwy fl    class
   <chr>        <chr>    <dbl> <int> <int> <chr>    <chr> <int> <int> <chr> <chr>
 1 audi         a4         1.8  1999     4 auto(l~  f        18    29 p     comp~
 2 audi         a4         1.8  1999     4 manual~  f        21    29 p     comp~
 3 audi         a4         2    2008     4 manual~  f        20    31 p     comp~
 4 audi         a4         2    2008     4 auto(a~  f        21    30 p     comp~
 5 audi         a4         2.8  1999     6 auto(l~  f        16    26 p     comp~
 6 audi         a4         2.8  1999     6 manual~  f        18    26 p     comp~
 7 audi         a4         3.1  2008     6 auto(a~  f        18    27 p     comp~
 8 audi         a4 quat~   1.8  1999     4 manual~  4        18    26 p     comp~
 9 audi         a4 quat~   1.8  1999     4 auto(l~  4        16    25 p     comp~
10 audi         a4 quat~   2    2008     4 manual~  4        20    28 p     comp~
# ... with 224 more rows
> |
```

Here is the code for creating a histogram from the above data:

```
library(ggplot2)
theme_set(theme_classic())

# Histogram for a Continuous Variable (Numeric)
gp <- ggplot(mpg, aes(displ)) +
scale_fill_brewer(palette = "Spectral")

gp + geom_histogram(aes(fill=class),
                    binwidth = .1,
                    col="black",
                    size=.1) +   # change binwidth
  labs(title="Histograms",
       subtitle="Engine Displacement")

gp + geom_histogram(aes(fill=class),
                    bins=5,
                    col="black",
                    size=.1) +    # changing the number
of bins
  labs(title="Histogram",
       subtitle="Engine Displacement")
```

This will generate the following histogram:

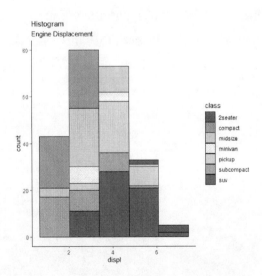

P u b l i c a t i o n - r e a d y   P l o t s

With the *ggpubr* package for R, one can create ggplot2-based graphs, which are good for researchers with minimal programming knowledge. Here is an example in which we are plotting a density distribution for the iris dataset. We are using the attribute "Petal.Length" and the coloring is done via the various species:

```
library(ggpubr)
ggdensity(iris, x = "Petal.Length",
    add = "mean", rug = TRUE,              # Add mean
line and marginal rugs
    color = "Species", fill = "Species",   # Coloring
based on groups
    palette = "jco")                       # use the
jco journal for color palette
```

The code will return the following density distribution:

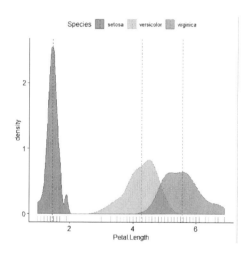

We may also choose to plot a scatter plot having *p*-values in order to compare the various groups. This is shown below:

```
# Groups to be compared
ourcomparisons <- list(
  c("setosa", "virginica"), c("setosa", "virginica"),
```

```
c("versicolor", "virginica")

)
# Create a box plot while changing colors via groups:
Species
# Adding jitter points then changing the shape via
groups
ggboxplot(
    iris, x = "Species", y = "Petal.Length",
    color = "Species", palette = c("#00AFBB",
"#E7B800", "#FC4E07"),
    add = "jitter"
    )+
    stat_compare_means(comparisons = ourcomparisons,
method = "t.test")
```

The code will return the following figure:

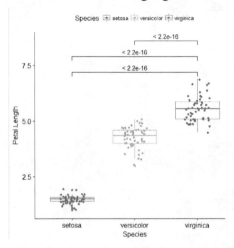

12-Data Science Software Tools

Computer programming is an important aspect of data science. It is a fact that an individual with sufficient knowledge in programming logic, functions, and loops has a higher chance of succeeding in data science. Python and R are the main programming languages used in data science and are used to create machine learning models that can draw patterns and make predictions based on the available data.

However, not everyone has studied computer programming. A number of people want to venture into data science but they don't have any programming knowledge. There are, however, a number of software tools for data science. These tools present the user with a graphical user interface (GUI) that they can use to create machine learning models without an in-depth knowledge of programming and algorithms. Let us discuss the software tools used in data science.

RapidMiner

This software was launched in 2006 as an open-source and stand-alone tool and given the name Rapid-I. It was later named RapidMiner and it has received funding over the years. All versions of the software below version 6 (v6) are open-source, but the later versions of the software come with a 14-day trial period. After 14 days, you must purchase the license.

The RapidMiner tool usually covers the whole life cycle of prediction modeling, including data preparation, model building, validation, and deployment. The GUI of the tool comes in the form of a block diagram and it is somehow similar to the MATLAB Simulink. It has a number of predefined blocks that work similarly to the plug-and-play devices. Your work is only to connect them in the correct order and you will be able to apply a number of algorithms to your data without writing a single line of code. It is also possible for you to integrate some custom R and Python codes into the software. The tool currently offers the following:

- RapidMiner studio - a stand-alone software that can be used for data preparation, visualization, and in statistical modeling.

- RapidMiner server - an enterprise-grade environment that comes with central repositories to facilitate team work, model deployment, and project management.

- RapidMiner Radoop - this provides the capabilities of big data analytics, which are centered on Hadoop.

- RapidMiner Cloud- this is a cloud-based repository that allows the easy sharing of information between the various devices.

Most industries are now using RapidMiner software. Examples of such industries include banking, automotive, insurance, manufacturing, life sciences, retail communication, oil, and gas.

This tool can be integrated with several sources of data including Oracle, Access, Excel, Microsoft SQL Server, MySQL, Ingres, Postgres, text files, dBASE, IBM SPSS, etc. The RapidMiner studio provides data scientists with a nice interface and allows them to create analysis interfaces without coding. The RapidMiner server allows sharing and collaboration among teams and is good for facilitating scalability and improved performance when the data scientist is running a complex analysis.

DataRobot

This is one of the best machine learning platforms available in data science. With this tool, you are only expected to provide the data and business knowledge, and the rest will be taken care of.

The DataRobot platform will automatically detect the best data pre-processing as well as feature engineering by employing the concept of text mining, encoding, variable type detection, scaling, imputation, transformation, etc. The hyper parameters are usually chosen automatically based on error-metric and validation set score.

The tool offers parallel processing. This is because the computation process is normally subdivided among thousands of available multi-core servers. Distributed algorithms are used for scaling large datasets. Deployment of the models is also easy with this tool as you are expected to make only a few clicks. If you are a software engineer, then you will have access to Python SDK and APIs for quick integration of the models into the software and tools.

BigML

This tool provides the user with a simple GUI and the user is expected to go through the following steps:

- Sources - Use various sources of information.
- Datasets - Use the sources so as to create a dataset.
- Models - Make predictive models.
- Predictions - Generate the predictions based on your model.
- Ensembles - Create an ensemble of the various models.
- Evaluation - Evaluate the model against the validation sets.

The above steps have to iterate in different orders. BigML platform provides data scientists with a nice visualization of the results and it has algorithms that can solve classification, clustering, regression, anomaly detection, and association discovery problems.

To use BigML, begin by signing up for a trial account. Before creating a model, you should first identify your data source or the place where you will get the data for training your model.

Google Cloud Prediction API

This tool provides RESTful APIs, which can be used for the construction of machine learning models to be used in android applications. This is basically a platform for mobile devices running the Android operating system. The following are some of the use cases for this tool:

- Recommendation engine - If you are given the user's past viewing habits, then predict the other movies or products the user might like.

- Sentiment analysis - Analyze the posted comments about a product to know their tone, whether positive or negative.

- Spam detection - Categorize your emails as either spam or not spam.

- Purchase prediction – Given a user's spending history, predict the amount they might spend on a particular day.

Although it is possible for any system to use this API, there exist some specific Google API client libraries that have been built to provide better security and performance. These exist for a number of programming languages including Python, Java, Go, JavaScript, Node.js, Ruby, PHP, and Objective-C.

Narrative Science

This software works by generating reports based on input data. It works in a similar manner as a data story-telling tool, which is highly used in advanced natural language processing for creating reports. The platform incorporates the following features:

- Some specific statistics and past organizational data.

- It helps generate personalized reports targeted at a

specific audience.

This tool is now widely used in insurance, financial, e-commerce, and government domains.

M L B a s e

This is an open-source project developed by Algorithms Machines People (AMP) lab at the University of California, Berkeley. The main idea behind the project is to provide an easy way to use machine learning to solve complex problems. This tool comes with the following:

- MLib - this works in a similar manner as the core distributed ML Library found in Spark. Although this was developed for the first time as part of the MLBase project, it is now supported in the Spark community.

- MLI - this is an experimental API used for algorithm development and feature extraction, and it introduces some high-level ML programming abstractions.

- ML Optimizer - this is a layer which helps in the automation of the process of constructing an ML pipeline. It usually solves search problems over ML algorithms and feature extractors included in MLlib and MLI.

This software is still under development, so you should expect new features to be implemented.

W e k a

This a tool developed with Java programming language and

commonly used in data science. The tool is open-source, and it provides an easy to use GUI, which is especially good for those who are beginners in data science.

The tool was developed at the University of Waikato, New Zealand, so as to be used in research. It features a collection of data mining tasks and machine learning algorithms. The software provides data scientists with tools for preprocessing, regression, classification, clustering, visualization, and association rules. Weka is a good tool for those in need of developing new schemes for machine learning.

Although Weka provides its users with a GUI, it is possible for you to use Java code so as to call it. You may ask yourself, what is the purpose of this feature? When you are working with large datasets, this can help automate your tasks. Because Java can be used for Hadoop, it is possible for you to use Weka for big data. To use this software, you have to download, install, and then start it. You will be provided with an easy-to-use GUI and you will accomplish your data science tasks.

For you to use this software, you have to visit the Weka Download Page and download from there. There are versions for Windows, Linux, and Mac OS X, so download the one suitable for your computer. Note that it requires you to have first installed Java in your computer. However, there are Weka versions that will install Java for you, so there is no need for you to have installed the Java in your computer. For Windows and Mac OS X, Weka provides an all-in-one version, which comes with the Weka platform that can be used for predictive modeling and a Java version, which you need so as to install Weka.

If you are using Windows, then double click on the package after download and the installation will begin. Follow the installation prompts correctly and the Weka will be added to the program menu. To start Weka, you have to click the "bird" icon.

For users of Mac OS X, the all-in-one version of Weka comes in the form of a disk image. This disk image has two Weka versions, one bundled with the Java version and the other is a stand-alone. It is good for you to install both. Drag the icon and folder into the Applications folder.

It is also possible for you to install Java and Weka separately. This is because you may have already installed the Java Development Kit or Java Runtime Environment in your computer. If this is the case, then you will have to download the Weka that has no Java. Double click on it to start the installation and its icon will be added to the Programs menu. However, for Mac OS, only one version of Weka is provided and this comes bundled with Java. To start Weka, you have to double click the Weka.jar file. It is also possible for you to start it from the command line.

Begin by changing the directory where you have installed Weka:

```
cd /Applications/weka-3-8-0
```
You can then launch the Java virtual machine as follows:
```
java -jar weka.jar
```

Automatic Statistician

This is a good tool for data exploration and analysis. The tool is capable of taking various types of data and using natural language processing so as to create a well-detailed report. When given data, this tool is able to find patterns and generate reports that companies can understand easily. In the report, data are described in terms of words and charts. This tool can help one find patterns that the data analyst cannot find. For example, this tool was provided with data on air travel and generated a nine-page report with four mathematical explanations detailing the trends identified in the data. These could be used in making predictions.

The tool features a collection of various statistical techniques that when combined can be used for building mathematical models. The tool usually selects the best model so as to generate the final report. Once you provide the data to this software, it will decide on its own the best model to use so as to generate the desired report.

Hadoop

This is a software framework that enables the distributed processing of large datasets contained across clusters. This is done by use of some simple programming models. Hadoop is liked for its low cost, flexibility, computation power, fault tolerance, and flexibility. It comes with the following modules:

- Hadoop common - contains common utilities responsible for supporting the other Hadoop modules.
- Hadoop Distributed File System - a distributed file system for providing high-throughput access to the application data.
- Hadoop YARN - this framework helps in scheduling

jobs and clustering the processes of managing resources.

- Hadoop MapReduce - this system is based on YARN and is used for processing large datasets.

Hadoop runs on the Linux operating system. If you are using other types of operating systems, then you can install VirtualBox and run Linux from it. The Hadoop file system should be separated from the Linux file system (this is why you should create a Hadoop user. This calls for you to use the "useradd" command so as to add the new user).

13-Programming Languages for Data Science

R for Data Science

R is a great programming language used for statistical computing and data analysis. Since its initial launch in the early 1990s, a lot of effort has gone into improving its interface. It started as a basic text editor to interactive R Studio and then to jupyter notebooks, and these have engaged many data scientists from all over the world.

R has benefitted a lot from its generous contributions by users from all over the world. Its many packages have also made it more powerful and liked by data analysts. Packages such as dplyr, tidyr, readr, data. table, SparkR, ggplot2, and others have made it easy for anyone to do data manipulation, computation, and visualization much faster.

Why Learn R?

1. R is a great programming language for data analysis. This is due to the following:

2. It provides an easy coding style.

3. R is open-source. You are not required to pay for any subscription.

4. It provides access to more than 7,800 packages that are customized for different uses.

5. It has overwhelming community support. You can get help from different online forums.

6. It offers a high-performance computing experience.

Installing R / R Studio

You can choose to use an old version of R, but it would be good for you to install and use R Studio. This is because it will provide you with better coding experience. To install R Studio, follow the steps given below:

1. Open

   https://www.rstudio.com/products/rstudio/download/ on your web browser.

2. In the "Installers for Supported Platforms" section, select and click the R Studio installer depending on your operating system. The download should begin immediately.

3. Click Next on every screen and, lastly, click Finish. You are now done.

4. To launch R Studio, click on its desktop icon or search it as "search windows" to access the program.

Installing R Packages

The power of R lies in its packages. It is the packages that let you perform the different data science tasks in R. To install a package, you must know its name. The installation can then be done by running the following command on the R terminal:

```
install.packages("package name")
```

The *package name* is the name of the package that you need to install.

Once the package has been installed, you will be able to use it to perform your data science tasks.

Python for Data Science

Other than R, Python is another programming language good for data science. Python has been in existence for a long time and has been used in many industries like oil, scientific computing, gas, physics, finance, signal processing, and many others. It has been used to develop applications like YouTube and it played a large role in powering the internal infrastructure of Google.

Why Learn Python?

The following are the reasons why you should learn Python for data science:

1. Python is a flexible and open-source programming language.

2. It is well known for its many libraries that can be used for data manipulation. Examples of such libraries include Pandas, Scikit-Learn, TensorFlow, PyTorch, NumPy, Scipy, and PyBrain.

3. The Cython library helps convert Python code to run in a C environment to reduce runtime and PyMySQL that helps in connecting to MySQL databases, extracting data, and executing queries.

4. Data analysis goes hand-in-hand with data visualization. Python has made a number of improvements to overtake its competitor, R, in data visualization. It has APIs likePlotly and libraries like matplotlib, Pygal, ggplot, NetworkX, and others for data visualization.

5. Python can also be integrated with other data visualization tools like Tableau and Qlikview using TabPy and win32com, respectively.

Installing Python

You can install and use Python on various operating systems including Windows, Mac OS X, and the various Linux distributions. The good news is that the newer versions of Linux come with Python installed, so you only have to update it if it is outdated.

To install Python on Windows or Mac OS X, just open the official Python website, which you can find by typing the following URL:

python.org

Click the Download button and choose the type of operating system that you are using. You will then be able to download the setup file with everything you need to get started with Python. Once the download is complete, double click the setup file to start the installation process. You will be taken through onscreen instructions and Python will be installed on your computer.

Installing Python Packages

To perform different data science tasks, we need to install packages. Python comes with the *pip* package manager, which make this easy. The *pip* package manager comes pre-installed in Python, meaning that once you install Python, you get *pip*.

Because we currently have Python 3.X, you can install a package by running the following command:

```
pip3 install package-name
```

The package will then be installed.

R vs. Python

R and Python are the main languages used for data science. Both are open-source languages with large community support.

However, despite this, Python has gained more popularity for use in data science tasks. The following points will help you know whether to choose R or Python for data analysis:

1. Use R when the data analysis is to be done on individual servers or in a stand-alone computing environment.

2. Use Python when you need to integrate the data analysis tasks with web apps or if you need to integrate the statistics code into a production environment.

3. R is easy for beginners and good for exploratory tasks. You can create a statistical model using only a few lines of code.

4. Python is good for implementing algorithms for use in a production environment.

5. R is good for data analysis because it provides numerous packages. One is also allowed to use formulas.

6. Python is an infant in data analysis, but its libraries have been updated, making significant improvements.

14-Applications of Data Science

With the increasing availability of huge amounts of data, companies have turned to data science for evidence-based decision making. Let us discuss the various areas in which data science is currently employed.

Transport

Some years ago in London, there was a need to handle more than

18 million journeys made by the soccer fans within London and

this issue was sorted out. TFL and train operators relied on data

analytics to ensure that nearly all the journeys were made

smoothly. They used data gathered from events and successfully

predicted the number of people that were to travel, which saw smooth transport within the city for athletes and spectators

travelling to and from the various stadiums.

Fraud Detection

This is regarded as one of the earliest applications of data analysis, with initial efforts being made from within the finance sector. The majority of organizations had been fed up with debt. They collected and stored a lot of data during the time customers were applying for loans and then applied data science to this data to save themselves from the losses that they had incurred.

In this way, banks learned how to divide and conquer data they get from their customers' profiles, their recent expenditures, and other information they can access. They can also determine or calculate the probability of having their customers default in making loan payments.

Policing/Security

A number of cities in the world have implemented predictive analysis systems to prevent crime in areas regarded as crime hotspots. This is normally done using both historical and geographical data. This has worked successfully in cities like London, Chicago, Los Angeles, etc. It is not possible for arrests to be made for each crime that is committed, but this has helped reduce the number of crimes committed in such areas due to police presence during peak crime periods. This way, we can have safer cities without putting the lives of police officers at risk.

Risk Management

The insurance industry is focused on risk management. Most insurers forget that during the process of insuring a person, the risk is not simply obtained from the data provided by the person but from the data analyzed statistically before making a decision. With data analytics, insurance companies can get actuarial data, claims data, and risk data, which are what it needs to consider before making a decision. An underwriter makes the evaluation before the individual is insured and an appropriate insurance policy and premium are set.

Nowadays, analytical software is used to detect various kinds of fraudulent claims. Red flag indicators are used for the identification of risky claims. This has made the claims process more efficient.

Web Provision

Most people tend to think that a "smart city" is any city with a fast internet speed provided by the government or companies operating from there and that people can use. This is good for any city, but it doesn't make it a smart city.

A city may have a fast internet connection, but this is just one of the things that can make it a smart city. The internet must be made available in the right place and access granted only to the right people. The internet should be able to shift the bandwidth at the right location and time. This is only possible through the use of data.

It is highly assumed that financial and commercial areas

should use high bandwidth during the weekdays. It is also assumed that residential areas should use high bandwidth during the weekends. This situation is more complex than it appears and it can only be solved through data analysis.

Speech Recognition

The best known speech recognition apps used worldwide are Google Voice, Siri, Cortana, and others. The use of voice recognition has made life easier for many. Imagine shutting the door of your living room while seated on your favorite couch or cleaning the house by just issuing a voice command, ordering for shopping from the supermarket while seated in your house, etc. All these have been made possible by data science and analytics algorithms.

With speech recognition, you only speak a message then it is converted into text. However, as you use speech recognition services, you will realize that sometimes it does not perform accurately.

Healthcare

Most countries have made significant improvements in providing quality healthcare to its citizens. This improvement has led to a rise in the cost of healthcare services as hospitals face the cost pressure of treating an increasing number of patients.

The use of machine and instrument data is on the rise in a bid to optimize and track treatment, the flow of patients, and the use of hospital equipment. It has been estimated that this will result in a

1% improvement in efficiency and result in savings of more than $63 billion in global healthcare services.

Internet/Web Search

When we hear the word "search," the word "Google" immediately clicks into our mind. Other than Google, there are several other search engines that you can use to search for what you want from the internet. Examples of such search engines include Bing, Yahoo, AOL, Duckduckgo, Ask, etc.

Each of the above engines works based on data science applications because algorithms are used for delivering the best results for any query that is posed within a second. Currently, Google alone processes more than 20 petabytes of data on a daily basis. If it were not for data analytics and data science, this would not be possible.

Digital Advertisement

Data science and analytics play prominent roles in running digital advertisements. All banners that you see on big websites and the digital billboards you see in big cities are controlled by the use of data analytics algorithms.

It is through the use of data analytics that digital advertisements get more clicks compared with the traditional way of running advertisements. When running digital advertisements, the target users are determined according to their previous behavior.

Recommender Systems

How can you forget the suggestions on similar videos on YouTube as well as suggestions of similar products on Amazon? These all rely on recommender systems, which are built using data science and analytics. These tools help you find the right product from billions of possible products while at the same improving the user experience.

Many companies have user recommender systems, also known as "recommender engines," to promote their products to potential customers in the form of suggestions to consumers based on their interests and relevant information. Some of the companies that use this system to improve the user experience include Amazon, Twitter, Netflix, LinkedIn, Google Play, imdb, and many others. The previous search results of the user are used for the purpose of making the necessary recommendations.

Gaming

By use of data analytics, EA Sports, Zynga, Nintendo, Sony, and Activision-Blizzard have taken the gaming experience to the next level. Machine learning algorithms have been used to develop games that upgrade/improve themselves as the player moves to the next higher level. When it comes to motion gaming, your opponent, that is, the computer, will analyze your previous moves and refine its game accordingly.

Conclusion

This marks the end of this book. Data science is a fast-growing field, especially due to new researchers and the increasing amount of data released by companies and organizations. There are also many open-source software products that can be used for data science and these have led to its increased popularity. Data science is a very promising field. This is because organizations are expected to collect/produce vast amounts of data over the next few years, meaning that data scientists will be able to access pools of data for research. Historical data are very important in data science in order to identify patterns that in turn can help make predictions. Businesses can take advantage of data science to create prediction models that can help them predict how their market will develop. Data science can also help businesses better understand their target audience. A business that utilizes data science in its decision making process has a higher chance of market success.

Fundamentals of Data Science